FIVE REASONS WHY MISTER P
IS THE BEST FRIEND TO HAVE:

He's really helpful(ish) . . .

He's great at sorting out problems—and he
can't even speak, so that's pretty amazing!

He gives the best bear hugs—although
sometimes he can squeeze a bit too tight
and his fur is a bit tickly!

He can do thirty-nine keepy-uppies!
How many can you do?

He's really funny and always makes you
smile—which is pretty much all you need in a

D0228388

'YOUR ATTENTION, PLEASE!' screeched the loudspeaker. 'COULD THE OWNERS OF A LARGE POLAR BEAR PLEASE MAKE THEIR WAY TO THE ICE-CREAM VAN AS QUICKLY AS POSSIBLE. THIS IS AN EMERGENCY!'

Arthur's eyes widened. He pulled Liam's arms away and ran as fast as he could towards the far end of the playing fields. Dad and Rosie and Tom ran with him. Before they got anywhere near the van, they heard a terrible commotion. A huge crowd was standing in a semi circle around the side of the van and they were shouting and laughing. Arthur pushed his way through. He emerged into the space in front of the crowd to find it littered with napkins and lollies and goodness knows what else.

'Mister P, what are you doing?' yelled Arthur, dodging a plastic lid as it flew through the air. Mister P had his snout plunged into a large tub of chocolate ice cream and, judging by the number of empty ice-cream tubs lying around him, this wasn't his first.

For Philip and Chiecco MF
For Florence DR

OXFORD
UNIVERSITY PRESS

Great Clarendon Street, Oxford OX2 6DP

Oxford University Press is a department of the University of Oxford.
It furthers the University's objective of excellence in research, scholarship,
and education by publishing worldwide. Oxford is a registered trade mark of
Oxford University Press in the UK and in certain other countries

First published 2017

British Library Cataloguing in Publication Data
Data available

ISBN: 978-0-19-274421-0

1 3 5 7 9 10 8 6 4 2

Printed in Great Britain

Paper used in the production of this book is a natural,
recyclable product made from wood grown in sustainable forests.
The manufacturing process conforms to the environmental
regulations of the country of origin.

ME
AND
MISTER P

WRITTEN BY
MARIA FARRER

ILLUSTRATED BY
DANIEL RIELEY

OXFORD
UNIVERSITY PRESS

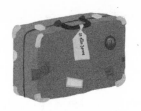

CHAPTER 1
SLAM!

Sent to my room AGAIN.

Today was supposed to be a good day, but it's turned into a bad day, so I'm stuck up here until my brother calms down. As usual, Liam is the one having a meltdown and, as usual, I'm the one sent upstairs. In my opinion this is one hundred per cent NOT FAIR. Some days I spend so much time upstairs that I think Mum and Dad forget I even exist.

Just for once I would like an ordinary day with an ordinary family and an ordinary brother.

Arthur stabbed the page a few times with his pencil, then checked the time. Ten minutes to go . . .

> I need Liam to calm down RIGHT NOW otherwise I will miss CITY'S football match on TV and if I miss even one second of the semi-final then I am done with this family FOR EVER.

Arthur underlined the words 'for ever' three times and then closed his journal. He'd been given it this week by the lady who came to visit the house to help with Liam things. She said Arthur could write anything in it and she promised no one would ever look at it. Arthur hoped this was true. He wouldn't like anyone to know what he really thought inside his head.

Arthur watched the seconds tick by. Five minutes to go until the semi-final started . . .

Four minutes . . .
Three minutes . . .

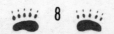

Arthur tried to imagine his favourite team coming out onto the pitch. Just two minutes now until the whistle went for the start of the game.

'Arthur,' Mum called from the bottom of the stairs, 'you can come down now. The football is about to start.'

'Is Liam going to watch?'

'Of course Liam is going to watch.'

Arthur groaned. He hid his journal in his very secret hiding place then ran down the stairs, taking the last five steps in one big leap. Liam was already sitting in front of the TV, so close that his nose was almost touching it. And he was humming. When Liam got excited, he liked to hum—which was sometimes OK, but usually not.

'Hey, Liam!' Arthur moved his chair to try to see past Liam's head. 'Shift over a bit, can't you? I can't see a thing.'

Liam ignored Arthur and started to hum more loudly. Arthur checked Mum was still in the kitchen and then pressed the volume control. Slowly the room filled with the sound of the crowd singing, clapping, and cheering.

Louder and LOUDER.

The atmosphere at the match was fantastic.

'Just six days left to enter our Funniest Football Photo Competition,' said the announcer. 'Three tickets to the cup final for the lucky winner.'

Arthur sighed. He'd give anything to win those tickets. One day, he dreamed of going to watch City play in the cup final, but his parents would never let him—it wouldn't be fair on Liam. Of course, Arthur would love to have a brother he could go to matches with—that would be the best thing in the world—but that brother was never going be Liam because even though Liam loved football, he hated strange places and crowds and noise. Arthur was fed up!

Arthur turned up the volume a little more. There was a

HUGE roar

and thunderous applause

as the teams ran out onto the pitch. Liam put his hands over his ears, rocked backwards and forwards, and moaned loudly, trying to drown out the sound. In seconds, Mum was in the room and grabbing the volume control.

'What are you doing, Arthur?' she whispered, pointing the control at the TV until the sound had died to nothing. 'You don't want to upset your brother again, do you?'

'But I don't want to watch the football with no volume. We *always* have to watch TV with no volume and it's no fun.'

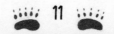

'Of course it's fun. It's no different really. You can still see what's going on.'

'I *would* be able to see what was going on,' whined Arthur, 'if Liam wasn't sitting right in front of the screen. And anyway, I want to *hear* what's going on. I don't want to listen to Liam humming the whole time. I need to listen to the commentary.'

Mum crouched down in front of Arthur and took his hands. 'Come on, Arthur. You have to try to understand what it's like from Liam's point of view.'

'I always have to understand Liam's point of view. What about MY point of view?' Arthur tried to grab the control back from Mum.

'Stop it!' shouted Mum. 'That's enough.'

Liam started to cry and Mum looked up at the ceiling and sighed.

'OK, that's it. No one is going to watch the football this afternoon.'

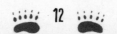

Mum turned off the TV and walked out of the room and into the garden.

Arthur couldn't believe it. 'This is all your fault,' he snapped at Liam. 'You can tell Mum and Dad I've had enough and I'm leaving this house and I'm not coming back.'

Liam covered his ears with his hands and cried even louder.

Arthur rushed up to his room, searched under his bed for his survival tin, and stuffed his lucky crystal into his coat pocket. Then he crashed down the stairs and flung open the front door. He barged past the polar bear who was standing on the doorstep and hurtled off down the street, running as fast as he could.

He wanted to get as far away from his house, his brother, and his stupid parents as possible. He wasn't going to let a polar bear or anything else stop him.

WAIT

ONE

SECOND!

HANG ON!

STO-O-O-OP!

Arthur slammed on the brakes so hard his trainers left burn marks on the pavement. A polar bear? On his doorstep? Was he imagining things? Arthur stamped on his own foot to make sure he wasn't dreaming. OUCH!

There was a polar bear—he was sure of it! Right on his doorstep! No way! Wow!

Now Arthur was in a dilemma. He wanted to run away, but he also wanted to check out the bear. Was it dangerous? Was it attacking his family at this very moment? Did he care? Arthur thought for a moment and decided perhaps he did. However annoying his family could be, he really didn't want them to be munched by a polar bear. Perhaps he could run away later? Right now it seemed more important to get back home. He spun around and . . .

'Waaaaaaahhhhhhh!'

'Grrrrrrr!'

The polar bear was so close that Arthur could feel its icy breath on his face. He was so close that he could see its shiny nose, its night-black eyes, its enormous claws. The bear took a step towards him.

'Waaaaaaahhhhhhh!'

Arthur yelled again, waving his arms in the air.

The bear stood up on its hind legs and waved its huge hairy paws back at Arthur.

This was bad. Very bad. This was double, triple, quadruple times worse than anything else that had ever happened.

Arthur pressed his lips together so another scream couldn't escape. He wondered if there was anything useful in his survival tin. His fishing hook and line? His earplugs? His fire-lighting kit? He was pretty certain a fire might scare away a polar bear, but how could he light a fire if he had no twigs or grass or anything? Arthur stood like a statue.

The bear stood like a statue. Inside Arthur's very still body, his ♥ was thumping and inside his very still head his mind was racing. He thought it best to seem friendly so he nodded and smiled at the polar bear. The bear nodded at Arthur and bared its long, sharp teeth.

Arthur was terrified. He tried to think of a plan, but he wasn't very good at plans and he'd never had to make one involving a polar bear before. He decided he needed to catch the bear unawares, dart past him, and run for home. It wasn't much of a plan but it was the best he could come up with. The trouble was, he wasn't exactly sure what made a bear unaware.

Arthur looked at the ground and the bear looked at the ground.

He looked at the sky and the bear looked at the sky.

Hmm, thought Arthur. He covered his eyes with his hands and, when he opened his fingers just enough to peep through, he saw the polar bear had covered its eyes with its paws—and Arthur was pretty certain that you couldn't peep through a paw.

This was Arthur's chance.

He'd run for it while the bear wasn't looking.

He tiptoed past the bear and then sprinted at top speed. He didn't stop to look over his shoulder. He didn't dare listen for the sound of huge paws

thud,
thud,
thudding

behind him.

He ran all the way home, as fast as his legs would carry him, let himself into his house, slammed the door, and flicked the lock on the safety latch. He leant against the door, breathing hard.

'Arthur, is that you?' Dad asked, poking his head round the living room door. 'Where have you been?'

'I ran away,' gasped Arthur, still out of breath. 'For EVER. Not that anyone noticed.'

Dad frowned and nodded. 'Well, I'm very glad you've decided to come back.' He gave a deep sigh. 'I know it's been a bad day—I do understand—but running away is not the answer. It really isn't. Apart from anything else it isn't safe.'

'Too right it's not,' said Arthur. 'There's a polar bear hanging around out there.'

Dad chuckled. 'Nice one, Arthur! Floated here on an iceberg, did he? Look, I'm sorry about the football. Perhaps we can watch the highlights later. Polar bear, eh?' Dad shook his head and disappeared back into the living room. 'No one can accuse you of not having a good imagination.'

Arthur didn't care about the football any more. He had BIGGER things to worry about—and it wasn't in his imagination. What if the bear came back to his doorstep? Now it had picked up Arthur's scent, who knew what it might do? He felt in his pocket for his lucky crystal, but the crystal wasn't there. He patted his other pocket—his survival tin had gone too. Oh no! They must have fallen out when he ran away and now his two most treasured possessions were lying somewhere out there in the street—with a bear. Could today get any worse?

The doorbell rang, once and then twice. Arthur froze.

'Could you see who's there?' called Mum.

'But what if it's the bear?'

'Don't be silly, Arthur. There aren't any bears round here.'

Arthur heard Mum and Dad laughing and that made him even grumpier.

He stared at the door, trying to make up his mind what to do. 'Who is it?' he called.

There was no answer.

He carefully lifted the flap of the letter box so he could peer out. He put his eyes to the opening and jerked back. Stuck right in the

opening—right there in front of his eyes—was a
long
    furry
        nose.

Arthur opened his mouth to scream, but no
sound would come out. He tried to move, but
his feet were stuck to the floor.

After a few seconds the nose disappeared. Everything was quiet apart from the sound of Arthur's heart beating. Arthur decided to risk another look. He bent down, peeped through the letter box, and blinked in disbelief. The polar bear was lying on the ground just outside, gazing at the door with its big black eyes. One paw was resting on Arthur's survival tin and in the other paw was an old brown suitcase with a name written on it in frosty white writing:

Mister P

Arthur frowned. Mister P? Was that the bear's name? And what was it doing with Arthur's survival tin? Arthur took a step back and tried to think. He heard movement outside the door.

Arthur tried to gulp away his fear.

'Who is it now?' called Dad from the sitting room.

'Um...' Arthur could hardly say it was the polar bear. Dad hadn't believed him earlier and he wouldn't believe him now.

Louder this time.

Arthur didn't know what to do. He watched in horror as two long black claws slid through the letter box, and then horror turned to amazement as his lucky crystal rolled down the claws and dropped, like a peace offering, onto the doormat. The claws disappeared and the letter box closed with a *clink*. Arthur picked up his crystal and turned it over in his hand. He couldn't help thinking that perhaps the bear was trying to tell him something—or at least trying to be friends. Maybe if Arthur opened the door, just a little, the bear would give him back his survival tin too.

Arthur trembled as he unclicked the latch and turned the door handle. Immediately the door swung open and Arthur was flattened against the wall. The bear must have been leaning against the door! And now half a ton of enormous polar bear had fallen into the hallway and thudded onto the hall floor, sending the suitcase and Arthur's tin spilling across the floor.

The bear clambered to its feet, gave a loud yelp, and started to whimper. It was holding its paw off the ground and looked as though it had been hurt.

'What is going on out there?' shouted Mum.

Arthur wriggled out from where he was squished behind the door. He needed to keep Mum out of this situation. He kept his eyes on the bear as he replied. 'I—er—stubbed my toe and then I dropped my stuff and now I'm just clearing it up.'

Arthur edged closer to the bear and crouched down to examine its foot. He could see his fishing hook sticking out of one of the bear's black paw pads. Arthur scratched his head. He couldn't send the bear away with a fishing hook in its paw. That would be cruel. He was going to have to do something.

The bear whimpered again as he pushed at the hook with his nose.

'It's OK,' Arthur whispered. 'I'll get that out for you.'

The bear blinked and stretched his head forward until the tip of his cold black nose touched the end of Arthur's nose. Arthur tried to stay calm. He didn't exactly feel afraid, but it was the first time ever that he'd been nose to nose with a polar bear.

CHAPTER 2
SHHHHHHHHH!

'You need to be quiet,' whispered Arthur.
'If my family discover a bear in the house,
they'll go crazy.'

The bear's black eyes twinkled.

'What on earth are you doing out there?'
called Dad from the living room. 'Who's at
the door?'

'Nothing . . . no one.' Arthur crossed his
fingers behind his back. He didn't like lying,
but what else could he do? Whichever way
he looked at it, a polar bear in the house was
100% going to cause trouble. Liam was

already having a bad day and throwing a bear into the mix definitely wouldn't help.

If Arthur was going to help the bear, he decided the best thing was to sneak it up to his room, get the hook out of its paw, then get it back out of the house without anyone noticing. But doing that wasn't going to be easy—or quiet.

Arthur motioned to the bear to stay still, then walked into the living room. Mum and Dad were watching Liam construct some monster spaceship out of Lego. All Arthur needed was a noisy way to distract them while he got the polar bear up the stairs. He thought of kicking Liam's spaceship, but that seemed a bit too cruel.

'No more bears then?' said Dad, smiling.

Arthur narrowed his eyes. 'Actually, there are hundreds of them,' he said, in his most menacing voice. 'And they're all coming to eat you.'

He made his hands into a claw shapes and roared at the top of his voice. Liam screeched in terror and leapt to his feet, knocking the wing off his spaceship in the process. Now there was no shortage of noise.

'What did you have to go and do that for?' said Mum. 'Just as Liam was playing quite happily.'

'Go to your room this instant,' said Dad, 'and do not come down until you are ready to apologize.'

Arthur was out of the room as quick as a flash, slamming the door behind him. For once in his life, he didn't mind being told off. He grabbed the bear's suitcase and pointed up the stairs, putting his finger to his lips and beckoning to the bear to follow. For a moment Arthur wondered if the bear would even fit between the wall and the bannister— or if the stairs might collapse under its weight.

It seemed to take for ever, but step by step, the HUGE animal

limped its way up and eventually

Arthur got it to the door of his bedroom and pushed it in.

Phew!

The polar bear's **massive** body filled every spare centimetre of the room and there was hardly any space for Arthur to move. Arthur bit his lip and frowned. This actually wasn't funny—he had a real live polar bear in his room and no way of escape. He must be **CRAZY!** He Squeezed around the edge of the bear, crawled onto his bed, and put the battered old suitcase on his pillow.

'Is this yours?' he asked.

The bear blinked three times.

'Is your name Mister P?'

The bear blinked again.

'Well, my name is Arthur—Arthur Mallows— in case you're interested.' Arthur thought it was better to be friendly before attempting to remove the fishing hook, especially looking at the length of Mister P's claws. 'Now, we just have to make your paw better and then you can go wherever it is you want to go.'

Mister P hung his head. Arthur wondered where the polar bear was going. He did seem to be a long, long way from the Arctic. Still, that was hardly Arthur's problem.

'OK,' said Arthur, sounding braver than he felt, 'show me your paw.' Arthur pointed at Mister P's paw and held out his hand.

Mister P looked questioningly at Arthur and lifted up his foot.

'That's it,' said Arthur. He was pleased that

the fishing hook wasn't the kind with nasty barbs on it. He started to tug gently at the hook and Mister P gave a low growl. Arthur stopped and took a shaky breath.

'It's going to hurt a bit, I'm afraid. And it's no good growling at me. I'm only trying to help. Close your eyes—Mum always says it's better if you don't look.'

Mister P laid his snout on Arthur's lap and squeezed his eyes tight shut. This time Arthur decided speed was the best policy and he whipped the hook out as fast as he could.

'There! Gone!' He held the hook in the air.

Mister P opened his eyes, examined his paw, then pulled back his lips in what Arthur hoped was a grin.

'OK. Good. Well, it was nice meeting you. If you'd like to follow me back down, I'll let you out.'

Arthur started to manoeuvre his way off his bed, but Mister P splayed himself flat on the floor, completely blocking the bedroom door.

Arthur swallowed.

'You have to move, Mister P. You can't stay in here. Haven't you got somewhere else you need to be?'

The bear didn't move.

'It's not that I'm being unfriendly,' said Arthur. 'But you don't know my family . . .'

The bear lifted his head in the air and sniffed towards his suitcase.

Arthur looked at the case. Maybe it would give him a clue as to where the bear had come from, or where he was going to. He turned the

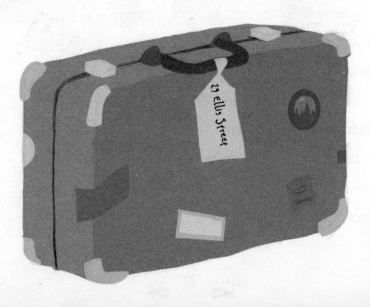

case over and spotted a small luggage label.

29 Ellis Street? But that was Arthur's address. Why would a polar bear have a suitcase with Arthur's address on it? Now Arthur was very curious. He undid the clips and lifted the lid just a crack. The smell was overpowering. It made his eyes water and he wrinkled up his nose as he tried not to breathe.

There was something very

fishy going on here.

Slowly he opened the case and clapped his hand over his mouth.

'YUCK!' Arthur thought he might be sick. 'Did you know you've got a dead fish in your suitcase?'

Mister P smacked his lips together.

'Oh no, no, no, no! You can't eat it! Not in here—in fact, not anywhere. I mean it's nearly rotten. We need to get rid of this thing before Mum and Dad get wind of it. It'll stink the whole house out.'

Holding his nose with one hand and gripping the slimy tail of the fish in the other, Arthur shuffled along his bed, trying not to get any stinky-fish-drips on his duvet. He opened his window, held the fish at arm's length, and was about to lob it out into the garden when Mister P lunged, sending Arthur's bedside light crashing to the floor. The bear grabbed the fish out of Arthur's hand, clamped it in its jaws, and started to devour it.

Arthur heard Dad's footsteps pounding up the stairs.

'What are you doing in there?' said Dad. 'Aren't you going to come down and apologize?'

Arthur watched his door handle turning

backwards and forwards as Dad tried to get in,
but Mister P's big backside was wedged right up
against the door and the door wouldn't budge—
not even a millimetre.

'Everything's fine, Dad—I'll be down soon.'

Mister P was busy licking every last scrap
of fish from the carpet and Arthur stared in
amazement at the bear's long blue tongue.

'And what is that terrible smell? Is it coming from your room?'

Even though Mister P had finished every last morsel of fish and was now busy licking up lumps of green fluff from the carpet, the smell was as strong as ever. Arthur couldn't think straight at all.

Dad hammered on the door again. 'Let me in. I know you're up to something.'

'I can't,' said Arthur. 'The door's jammed.'

'Well, un-jam it then.' Dad grunted and heaved against the door with his shoulder. 'Right, young man. If you're not going to let me in, then we'll have to do this another way.'

Arthur wondered what Dad could possibly do. He found out a few minutes later when there was a clatter as a long metal ladder clanked against the wall outside his bedroom window. Arthur looked around in a panic. He needed to hide Mister P.

He flung his duvet over the bear and did his best to cover him up, but the duvet wasn't nearly big enough, with

Mister P's big bum clearly visible at one end and his nose at the other.

Clunk, clunk, clunk,

went Dad's feet on the rungs of the ladder.

Mister P grumbled quietly and then gave a rasping

cough. Arthur hoped the bear wasn't about to cough up all the rotten fish he'd just eaten.

Clunk, *clunk, clunk.*

First the top of Dad's head appeared. And next Dad's whole face filled the open window. Arthur waved and smiled and pretended to read a book. Dad frowned and peered in. He looked—and then looked again.

'WHAT is that?' said Dad, pointing at the furry nose sticking out from under a mountain of duvet.

Before Arthur had time to answer, Mister P lifted his head off the ground, made another strange sound in his throat, and then coughed violently. A ball of fishy carpet fluff flew through the open window, just missing Dad's face.

Dad lurched backwards, pulling the ladder away from the wall. He reached for the window-ledge, trying to regain his balance, but it was too late. The ladder swayed from side to side and then started to tip. Dad shrieked and desperately tried to cling on.

Quick as a flash, Mister P pounced and hooked his claws through Dad's belt,

just as the ladder went clattering to the ground.
Dad was left hanging in mid-air, arms spiralling,
legs dangling.

'Aaaaaahhhhhhhhh!'

he screamed.

'Grrrrrr,'

Mister P growled, showing
his big white teeth. Dad's
eyes opened wide.

'Lizzie!' he called to Mum. 'Help me! Quick!'

Mum rushed into the garden. 'Oh my goodness, oh my goodness,' she cried, as she struggled to get the ladder back into position.

From somewhere downstairs, Arthur could hear the sound of Liam panicking. This was getting way out of control.

Mum steadied the ladder against the wall. Mister P carefully released Dad and watched as he clambered shakily down. Dad sat on the ground, mumbling incoherently and pointing up at the window.

'What are you talking about, Richard?' said Mum, examining Dad's head as if he must have hit it. 'What do you mean Arthur's got a *bear* in his bedroom?'

'Can't you see it?' gasped Dad. 'Up there!'

Mum looked up at the window, clapped her hand over her mouth, and sat down next to Dad.

'I tried to tell you earlier,' shouted Arthur. 'But you wouldn't believe me.'

'Are you all right, Arthur?' shouted Mum. 'Don't panic. I'll ring the police.'

'I'm not panicking,' said Arthur. 'And don't ring the police. Mister P won't hurt anyone. He's nice . . . and he just saved Dad's life, remember?'

'But he's a BEAR for goodness' sake. And how do you know his name?'

Arthur held up Mister P's case. 'It's on his suitcase.'

There was a long silence.

'I think I need a cup of tea,' said Dad. 'I'm feeling a bit faint.'

Dad didn't look good at all. He'd gone a kind of greyish colour. Mum looked from Arthur to Dad as if trying to decide who was in more trouble. Arthur decided to take control.

'You sort out Dad. Me and Mister P will be down in a minute.'

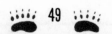

'And you're quite sure you're not in ANY danger?'

Arthur looked at Mister P who was sitting quietly beside him. He'd never seen a more un-dangerous looking polar bear in his whole life.

'Relax,' Arthur shouted down to Mum, 'we're cool.'

Mum didn't look the slightest bit relaxed as she hooked her arm through Dad's and supported him as he walked unsteadily back to the house. Arthur flopped down on his bed—he was feeling a little light-headed himself. He hoped Dad was OK. It must have been a shock falling off a ladder and being rescued by a polar bear. Arthur's eyes drifted back to the address label on Mister P's suitcase.

'I wonder what you're doing at my house, Mister P? Why have you come?'

Mister P touched him gently with his enormous paw.

'You want to be friends, don't you? I think

you'd like to stay.'

Mister P blinked three times.
Arthur stroked his paw and then shook it up
and down.

'This is how us humans shake hands—it's
what you do when you meet someone for the
first time. If I introduce you to Mum and Dad
and they see you're a polite polar bear, they
might let you stay—just for tonight. I'm not

making any promises. It's not that Mum and Dad are unfriendly, but you have to understand that we're not used to having bears round here.'

Poor Mister P looked tired and confused. Perhaps Arthur's house was his last hope? Arthur certainly hoped he could make Mum and Dad understand.

CHAPTER 3

BRRRRMMMMMM!

'Watch out, he's coming down!' shouted Arthur.

It had taken a little while for Arthur to get Mister P into a position where they could both get out of the bedroom. Now Mister P stuck out his front legs and slid down the steep stairs on his tummy like a polar bear on a snow slope.

Brrrrmmmmmm!

When he reached the bottom he skidded across the wooden floor and stopped just before his nose hit the front door.

Brrrrmmmmmm!

Mum and Dad peeped round the kitchen door, their faces stiff and serious. There was a moment's silence as Mister P got to his feet and gave himself a shake. Even Arthur had to admit, he was HUGE.

'This is Mister P,' said Arthur. 'Mister P, this is Mum and Dad.'

Mister P held out his paw like Arthur had taught him, but Mum and Dad shrank back behind the door.

'He's trying to shake hands,' said Arthur.

Dad swallowed hard and Mum gave a little wave. Liam was moaning quietly in the far corner of the kitchen.

Mister P cocked his head on one side to listen.

'That's my brother, Liam,' said Arthur. 'Don't worry—it might take a little while for them to get used to you.'

Mister P took a step towards the kitchen door.

'You're not coming in here,' said Dad, squaring up to Mister P with his arms outstretched.

Mister P twitched his nose and sat down.

'Mister P's suitcase has our address on it. I don't think he's got anywhere else to go so I'm wondering if we could let him stay. Just for tonight.' Arthur passed the case to Mum and Dad and pointed at the label.

'Did you write this, Arthur?' said Mum, examining it.

'No, I didn't. I promise. And we need to look after him because he's tired and he's hurt. Pleeeease.'

'Hurt?' said Mum, little lines of anxiety appearing on her face.

'He can hardly walk.' Arthur pointed at Mister P's foot.

Mister P held his bad paw in the air and moaned quietly. For a polar bear he was a pretty good actor.

Mum's face softened. 'Oh, you poor bear,' she said. 'What do you think, Richard? He does seem to be very polite. Maybe he could stay tonight and then we'll call the RSPCA in the morning. I doubt there'll be anyone there at this time on a Sunday anyway.'

Dad covered his face with his hands. 'Well, if he's going to stay, he'll have to go in the garage. I'm not sure Liam would cope with having a bear in the house.'

'We could put Liam in the garage instead,' said Arthur.

As soon as the words were out of his mouth, Arthur wished he could grab them back. He didn't mean to be horrible about his brother, not really. He knew it upset Mum and Dad and if he was going to negotiate for Mister P to stay, he needed Mum and Dad in a good mood, not a bad mood.

'I'm sorry,' said Arthur. 'I suppose you're right. Mister P can go in the garage. It's only that it's dirty and full of cobwebs, and I'm not sure he'll like it very much.'

'Well, if you're that worried, you'll just have to clean it up,' said Dad.

'But it's not *my* garage,' said Arthur grumpily.

'But it is *your* bear,' said Dad. 'So that makes it *your* problem.'

It's my family that's the problem, more like, thought Arthur to himself, then immediately

felt guilty. It seemed as though there
was no option but to set to work on the
garage.

Arthur filled a bucket with soapy water
and put it down in front of Mister P.

'You bring that,' he said, 'and I'll get
the broom.'

Mister P picked up the bucket in his
teeth and made a show of limping towards
the garage door behind Arthur. Arthur
could feel Mum and Dad watching and he
hoped they were feeling sorry for him.

He opened the back door of the garage—the one that led from the garden—and turned on the light. It was even worse than he thought. There were cobwebs and dust everywhere and the windows were covered in a mossy green grime. He didn't reckon Dad had cleaned it EVER.

'Don't worry,' said Arthur, scratching Mister P behind the ears. 'We'll make it cosy. You can help me clean the windows. You do the outside and I'll do the inside.'

He handed Mister P a cloth, and Mister P plunged it into the bubbles and started scrubbing away at the grubby glass. Soon Arthur and Mister P could see each other clearly through the window. Mister P pressed his face hard against the glass, squishing his nose and baring his teeth. Arthur did the same back. One look at Arthur's little teeth and Mister P started rolling around on the grass. Arthur was pretty certain he was laughing.

'Come on, stop messing around, we're not finished yet,' said Arthur. 'You need to get back in here and help me get rid of all these cobwebs.'

As Mister P plodded into the garage it was clear he wasn't so keen on the cobwebs. He grizzled as they stuck to his fur and got caught round his claws. Then, suddenly, he froze. His fur stuck up on end and he snarled. Right in front of his nose was an enormous, black, long-legged . . .

SPIDER!

The spider stayed still as Mister P moved closer and closer. Then the spider scuttled straight at Mister P's nose. Mister P leapt backwards, turned a circle, and was out of the garage and down the end of the garden before Arthur had time to say a word. It was hard to believe a polar bear could be such a coward.

Arthur scooped the spider into the cup of his hand. 'Sorry, mate, but you're going to have to leave. I'll never get that silly bear back into the garage if he thinks you're here.'

He carried the spider into the garden and tipped it over the fence. Mister P covered his eyes with his paws.

Arthur shook his head and returned to the garage. He swept the floor then looked around. The garage was clean and spider-free, but it didn't look very comfortable. He bit his lip and wondered what would make a polar bear feel at home. A rug, maybe? Some pillows? A friend so he didn't get lonely?

Arthur ran upstairs to see what he could find. He grabbed a blanket from the top of his cupboard and his spare pillow. Then he pulled out his old cuddly toy from under the bed—his very special, favourite, scruffy old monkey, the one that he'd pretended he had lost so that no one would think he was silly. Bingo would make the perfect friend for Mister P.

Arthur tucked Bingo under one arm and the blanket and pillow under the other and carried them down to the garage. He spread the blanket on the floor and put the pillow at one end with Bingo sitting against it.

'Come and see,

Mister P,'

called Arthur.

Mister P was nervous about returning to the garage and checked every corner for spiders before settling himself down on the blanket. Arthur tucked Bingo into the crook of Mister P's leg and within minutes the bear was snoring VERY loudly!

Arthur sat and watched. He heard a faint humming sound and turned to see Liam shuffling in through the doorway. Liam stood with his back to the wall

and stared at Mister P for ages and ages.
'You can say hello to him if you like, Liam.
He won't hurt you.'
Liam took a step towards the bear. Mister P
opened one eye and Liam legged it out of the

garage before Arthur could stop him.
Arthur sighed and sat down next to Mister P.
He leant against his warm, furry body. 'Don't

worry about my brother,' he said. 'You don't
need to take any notice of him.'

Mister P grumbled quietly.

'I know, that's what I feel like a lot of the
time,' said Arthur. 'Not that anyone in this
family really cares about what I feel. The only
one they care about is Liam.'

Mister P curled himself around Arthur and
Arthur laid his head on the bear's soft tummy.
He wished Mister P could stay for ever.

CHAPTER 4

HISSSSSS!

Monday mornings in Ellis Street tended to be
noisy—and not in a good way. Liam didn't
like changes to his routine and getting him into
school at the beginning of the week was a bit of
a struggle. Arthur was used to waking up to the
sound of Liam yelling in the next door room. It
made Arthur sad and angry all at the same time
and he'd bury his head under his pillow to block
out the sound.

This Monday morning, though, it was
strangely quiet and that made Arthur think
something must be up. He raced downstairs in
his pyjamas.

The door to the garden was open and Mum was sitting on the step sipping tea. Mister P was up and out of the garage. Liam was dressed in his school uniform and was sitting astride Mister P's back, riding round and round the garden.

Arthur was speechless. The bear was HIS friend. Mister P hadn't offered to give him a ride so why was Liam getting to have all the fun? Liam didn't even like Mister P, did he? Arthur walked back into the house and slammed the door behind him. He went upstairs, got dressed for school, and ate breakfast in the kitchen by himself. Every now and again, he glanced out of the window. Liam and Mister P were still going round and round and Arthur got angrier and angrier.

'Morning, Arthur,' said Mum cheerfully. 'Did you get out of bed on the wrong side?'

'Have you rung the RSPCA yet?' asked Arthur.

Mum shook her head and pointed to the window. 'Well, no, I haven't. Liam seems very comfortable with Mister P. They're getting on very well, and this is the best Monday morning we've had in ages. I think it might be good if Mister P stayed for a couple more days, don't

you? That'll give his paw time to fully recover.
Perhaps the two of you could take him to
school?'

'*I* could take him to school. Mister P doesn't
belong to Liam. He's mine.'

'I'm not sure Mister P belongs to anyone,' said
Mum. 'And you should be pleased your brother
and Mister P are getting on so well. It's nice.'

'Nice for Liam and Mister P,' said Arthur.
'Not nice for me.'

Mum frowned and gave Arthur a hug. 'I
thought you wanted Mister P to stay,' she said.

Arthur kicked at the table leg. Of course he
wanted Mister P to stay.

Mum looked at the clock. 'Well, come on
then, it's time to get going. We wouldn't want
Mister P to be late for his first day at school.'

Arthur nodded.

Liam stayed on Mister P's back all the way
out to the driveway and then he slid off and
stood by him.

Arthur looked at their car . . .

and then

at Mister P.

He wasn't that good at maths but even Arthur's rough calculations suggested that trying to get a **very large** polar bear into the back seat of Mum's car was not going to be an easy task. He opened the car door.

'In you get,' said Arthur, trying to sound optimistic.

Mister P shook his head and backed away.

'You want to come to school don't you? Think SMALL.'

Mister P blinked at Arthur and sidled up to the car. First he tried reversing in. He wedged his back end through the door and tried to wriggle it into the back seat.

'Breathe in!' said Arthur.

Mister P gasped.

Arthur pushed

and

pushed, but it was no good.

There had to be an easier way.

They started again. This time Mister P tried climbing in nose first. He w r i g g l e d and **heaved** his way across the back seat. He managed to get one of his back legs in, but the other was still dangling

outside.

Now the roof of the car was bending upwards in a dome and the floor of the car was almost touching the ground.

'STOP!'

cried Mum.

'My car is going to fall to bits, if you carry on like this.'

'I could take him on the bus,' said Arthur. 'There'd be plenty of room for a polar bear on the bus.'

Arthur hadn't been allowed to take the bus since the day Liam started coming to his school. Mum and Dad said the bus was too noisy and too crowded for Liam so now they had to go in the car. Arthur hated being driven to school when all his friends were on the bus. He felt pathetic. And he hated arriving at school with Liam and having to walk across the playground with him. He always got the feeling some people were watching just to see if Liam did anything weird. And Arthur didn't like that feeling. In fact he hated having Liam at school with him full stop. Not that he'd ever tell anyone because those are the kinds of thoughts you keep to yourself.

'All right—good idea,' said Mum, searching in her purse for some money. 'But you'll have to run. The bus is due any minute.'

'**Yesss!**' Arthur punched the air. 'Come on, Mister P. You're coming on the bus with me.'

Mister P set off at a trot behind Arthur. Arthur could see the bus coming up the road. 'Faster, Mister P!' he shouted. 'We don't want to miss it.'

Mister P pounded along the pavement, huffing and puffing. They reached the stop just as the bus pulled in.

The doors opened with a pop and HISSSSSS!

Mister P jumped back, covering his ears. He looked terrified.

'It's OK,' said Arthur, soothingly. 'It's just a bus door.'

Mister P examined the door carefully, pushing

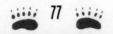

it with his paw and sniffing.

'I can't wait all day,' said the driver. 'You'll mess up my schedule. On or off, make up your mind.'

'Sorry,' said Arthur. 'I think it's Mister P's first time on a bus.'

'Well, it's a first for me too,' said the driver. 'Never had a polar bear on board before. Come on, Mister whatever-your-name-is. On you get, we'll look after you.'

Arthur pushed Mister P onto the bus and got out his money. The bus driver scratched his head. He wasn't sure how much he should charge for a bear, so he thought it best to let him travel for free.

As Mister P squeezed along the aisle towards the back of the bus, everyone edged into their seats to get out of his way. People muttered and complained as he knocked school bags off the seats, spilling books onto the floor.

'Sorry, sorry, sorry,'

Arthur apologized to fellow passengers, as he followed the bear along the bus, picking up the bits behind him. He was relieved to see his friend Tom sitting near the back. Tom looked very excited as he beckoned to Arthur to come and join him. Mister P seemed excited too and grinned happily at the passengers on the bus, showing all forty-eight of his razor-sharp teeth. Everybody **gasped**. One of the younger children started to cry.

'Settle down, please,' called the driver.

There was a bigger space in the middle of the bus where people could stand if things got crowded.

'You lie down here,' said Arthur. 'Keep your mouth shut and stay still.'

Mister P turned a couple of circles and then plonked himself down on the floor with a loud **hrrrrmph**. Arthur made his way to a seat next to Tom.

'What in the world is that?' whispered Tom,

pointing to Mister P.

'It's a polar bear, stupid. He's come to stay for a while and we couldn't get him in the car.'

'Why would a polar bear want to stay with you?' said Elsa. 'No one likes coming to your house.' Elsa was mean and horrible and definitely not one of Arthur's mates.

'Mister P likes staying at our house,' said Arthur.

'Well, he'd have a much better time staying with me,' said Elsa. 'For a start he wouldn't have to put up with your weirdsville brother.'

Arthur's cheeks burned and tears pricked at his eyes. 'My brother is *not* weirdsville and, for your information, Liam and Mister P get on very well. You don't know anything.' Arthur hated it when other people were mean about Liam. It felt like they were being mean to *him*.

Elsa started laughing and flapping her hands.

Mister P lifted his head and snarled. Elsa looked scared and Arthur was glad.

'Anyway,' she said, 'I wouldn't want your bear in my house because his breath stinks of fish. I can smell it from here.'

Mister P growled louder. Elsa turned her head away and stared out of the window.

At that moment the doors hissed shut, and the bus juddered forward. Mister P jumped up and lurched towards the back of the bus, falling onto his knees, his nose ending up right in Elsa's face.

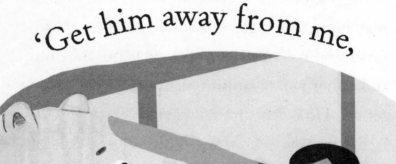

'Get him away from me,

get him away from me!' squealed Elsa, as she tried to bash Mister P over the head with her bag.

'Stop it,' shouted Arthur.

'You're scaring him.'

But Elsa did NOT let up.

The bus came to an unscheduled stop.

'Right,' said the driver, getting out of his seat, 'I suggest everyone calms down. A polar bear may be an unusual passenger, but he's got as much right as the rest of you to travel on a bus and either you treat him nicely or you'll have to get off. Do I make myself clear?'

Elsa crossed her arms and frowned. 'This bus is way better when you and your smelly friend aren't on it,' she said to Arthur.

'Come on,' said Tom. 'I've had enough. Let's move forward so we don't have to listen to her—' he nodded towards Elsa—'and it'll be easier to look after Mister P.'

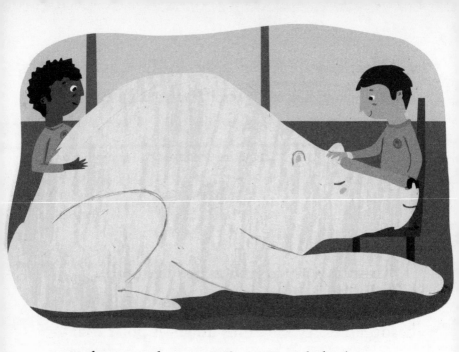

Arthur sat close to Mister P and the bear
put his head on the seat beside him. Tom sat
opposite. At the next stop, the two boys did
their best to keep Mister P calm as the doors
hissed open and shut. Luckily only one person
got on and Arthur was glad to see it was Rosie.

Rosie was very nice and very clever. She was
also the best player on Arthur's football team.
She always wore a large pair of headphones on
the bus so she could read her book in peace.

'Wow!' she said, as she stared at Mister P.

She edged into the seat beside Tom and took off her headphones. 'What a beautiful bear. Why's he looking so sad?'

'He's scared of the noise the bus doors make,' said Arthur.

'And he doesn't like Elsa,' said Tom, 'because she's being mean, as usual.'

Rosie frowned at Elsa and Elsa scowled. 'Perhaps Mister P would like to borrow my headphones,' she said, 'then he won't be able to hear Elsa or the doors or anything else.'

Rosie held out her headphones to Mister P. He looked at them carefully and gave them a lick.

'You don't eat them,' Rosie laughed. 'You put them on your ears, like this.'

Rosie held one of the earphones by Mister P's ear and hung her iPod round his neck. Arthur could hear the music playing.

Mister P blinked and gave his head a little shake. Then he started to tap one paw on the seat in time to the music. Rosie gently slipped the headphones over Mister P's ears. His nose nodded from side to side and he made a strange whining noise in his throat.

'He's trying to sing!' said Tom, laughing.

'Out of tune,' said Elsa.

'So where did he come from?' asked Rosie.

'He just kind of arrived on the doorstep.'

'But how?' asked Tom.

'And why?' asked Rosie.

Arthur shrugged.
He'd been
wondering the
same himself.

CHAPTER 5
SLURP!

Arthur pretended not to notice Mum and Liam
waiting at the school gates. As the bear jumped
down from the bus, Liam hopped up and down
and started to hum loudly. Mister P was still
wearing Rosie's headphones and his bum swayed
from side to side, and as he danced towards
Liam, Liam began to dance along with him.
Arthur was beginning to wonder if bringing a
polar bear to school was such a good idea after
all. He hung his head and wished he could jump
into a hole in the ground.

'Relax,' said Tom. 'They're just having some
fun.'

'But people will laugh,' replied Arthur.

'Well, you have to admit, a polar bear dancing is pretty funny.'

Arthur shrugged. He knew he could be over-sensitive about Liam, and when he looked up, he saw Tom was right. Everyone was pointing at Mister P and Mister P didn't seem to mind one bit. Liam went happily all the way to his classroom and Arthur had to admit this was a good result for a Monday morning. As soon as he was sure Liam was OK, he tugged Mister P towards his own classroom and removed the headphones from his ears. They paused at the door before going in.

'Now, be sensible,' said Arthur. 'And no grinning or you'll scare Mr Craddock.'

Arthur's teacher, Mr Craddock, did not like unforeseen circumstances. In Mr Craddock's opinion, a polar bear arriving in his classroom on a Monday morning was a prime example of an unforeseen circumstance—and a dangerous one at that. The minute Mister P walked in, Mr Craddock dropped the books he was carrying and herded the class into one corner of the room, standing in front of them with his arms outstretched.

'Keep calm, everyone,'
said Mr Craddock
in a shaky voice.
'KEEP CALM!'
But no one was calm—particularly not Mr
Craddock—and as the noise in the classroom
got louder and louder, Mister P got more and
more restless. Arthur tried to explain that
Mister P was a friendly bear, but Mr Craddock
was far too busy making a barricade out of
tables and chairs to listen. Mister P started
prowling up and down the
barricade, swiping at it
with his paw. Arthur did
his best to keep Mister P
under control, but the
bear didn't really
understand. The
louder the
commotion in the
classroom, the

more anxious Mister P became until finally he stood on his hind legs and ROARED.

'Help!' shouted Mr Craddock at the top of his voice. 'HELP!'

In a nanosecond, the headteacher, Mrs Barnes, appeared at the door and everyone went quiet, including Mister P.

'Goodness gracious,' she said. 'What is going on in here, Mr Craddock?'

Mr Craddock trembled behind his barricade and pointed at Mister P.

Arthur stepped forward. 'Mrs Barnes, this is Mister P. He is a polar bear.'

Mister P held out his paw, just as Arthur had taught him, and Mrs Barnes shook it enthusiastically. 'Very pleased to meet you, Mister P,' said Mrs Barnes. 'Welcome to our school.' Arthur reckoned Mister P was going to like Mrs Barnes A LOT.

Then Mrs Barnes turned her attention to the barricade.

'Are we studying construction in Room 5B this morning, Mr Craddock?'

'Well, no, n-n-n-not exactly. It's just that ummm . . .' Mr Craddock nodded towards Mister P with his head. Mrs Barnes raised an eyebrow and waited but Mr Craddock seemed to have forgotten what he was going to say.

'This school welcomes diversity, Mr Craddock. It is a privilege to have a polar bear in our midst and I am sure we can learn as much from him as he can from us. We should be working to make our new and very special guest feel comfortable and welcome and not as if he's in some kind of zoo.'

'Which is where he *should* be,' said Mr Craddock.

Mrs Barnes gave him a frosty look. 'Let's put the classroom back in order and get to work as usual, shall we?' she said.

Mister P helped push the tables and chairs into place and Mrs Barnes made everyone sit down quietly. 'Now, some of you may not have spent much time with a polar bear before, so if there is anything we need to know, anything that might help Mister P to settle in, I'm sure Arthur will tell us.'

Arthur blushed. He wasn't sure he knew much more than anyone else. He'd only been living with Mister P for a day. And Mister P seemed to be settling in just fine. He had made his way to the front and was busy sniffing Mr Craddock's socks, which was making Mr Craddock even more nervous. Arthur wondered if perhaps Mr Craddock's feet smelt fishy.

'The thing is,' Arthur began, trying to pull Mister P away from Mr Craddock without any success. 'The thing is that when you are with Mister P you have to be . . . to be . . . flexible.' Arthur remembered this word from the lady who came to their house to work with Liam. 'You have to learn to watch out for what makes him happy and what makes him scared or angry because polar bears can sometimes be a little bit unpredictable.'

'That is very helpful,' said Mrs Barnes.

Mister P had started to lick Mr Craddock's shoes and Mr Craddock looked as if he might faint. A few people giggled. Arthur wished Mister P would stop embarrassing him. He gave Mister P a sharp nudge in the ribs.

'Sometimes Mister P gets scared if he doesn't understand what is going on, or if there's a noise he doesn't like, or if he sees a spider. And when he gets scared or upset he sometimes growls or roars. Other times he is happy and he grins— which looks scary but really isn't.'

Mister P stopped sniffing Mr Craddock's feet and gave a *big toothy grin.*

'Well,' said Mrs Barnes, 'while we have Mister P here, I think it would be a great opportunity for the whole school to do a special project on polar bears and see what we can discover about this amazing species.'

Mister P sat up very straight and looked rather pleased with himself.

After some discussion between Mrs Barnes and Mr Craddock, the class built Mister P a den in the reading corner. Mrs Barnes took a group to the school library to find books on the Arctic

and carried them back to the den. Mister P lay on the beanbags and helped the students to discover piles of interesting polar bear facts. He let them measure his paws and study his fur and count his teeth.

Mr Craddock gave a short presentation about how global warming was causing the sea ice to melt in the Arctic and making life very hard for polar bears. Mister P nodded wisely and gazed at Mr Craddock as if he was the best teacher on earth. At the end, Mister P stood up and clapped his paws together. The class joined in and Mr Craddock bowed his head and thanked Mister P for helping to highlight this very serious problem. Mister P bowed his head back, then turned and gave Arthur what looked like a wink. Arthur smiled.

By the end of the day, the whole school was talking about Mister P and the Arctic and climate change and sea ice. Arthur felt very proud of his bear. Mrs Barnes gave Arthur's class a merit award for helping Mister P to settle in to school and Mr Craddock  gave Mister P a gold star and a tin of sardines for being kind and co-operative. He said he hoped he'd come back again tomorrow.

After such a long and exhausting day, Mister P fell fast asleep on the bus. Everyone tiptoed around him, taking care not to wake him up. Finally, at Arthur's stop, Mister P clambered sleepily off the bus and plodded home. He went straight to the garage and lay down on his blanket.

'How was your day?' asked Dad, as Arthur flopped onto a chair in the kitchen.

'Interesting,' said Arthur.

'Interesting good or interesting bad?'

'Both.' And Arthur started to tell Dad about all the things that had happened that day— about the bus and the barricades and the project and all the excitement at school and how Mister P had eaten fish and chips and a whole tub of chocolate ice cream at lunch time.

'I suppose he's got a lot to learn,' said Dad. 'Do you think he's come to stay for long?'

Arthur shrugged. He didn't want to think about Mister P leaving—he'd only just arrived.

A few minutes later, the front door banged open and Liam struggled in carrying a blue plastic bucket. He was breathing hard and hyper-excited.

'What have you got there?' said Dad, trying to help. Mum shook her head.

'Fish,' said Liam, turning his back. He wouldn't let anyone touch the bucket.

'Fish?' asked Dad.

'For Mister P,' he said, as he heaved the bucket towards the garage.

'Liam's been studying the diet of a polar bear,' said Mum. 'His teacher showed me his work. He was determined to find a seal, a whale, or a walrus to bring home for Mister P. Luckily the fishmonger gave us a bucket of old fish that he was about to throw out. It was the closest we could get.'

Arthur, Mum, and Dad followed Liam and watched from the garage doorway as he put the bucket down and lifted the lid. Mister P dived into the bucket, his huge head completely disappearing. He chomped and guzzled until the bucket was empty and then sat down in front of Liam, his nose about two centimetres from Liam's nose.

Arthur held his breath, wondering how Liam would react with Mister P's fishy face so close to his. Mister P raised his paw and held it out towards Liam. Slowly Liam raised his hand and moved forwards until his palm was touching the bear's enormous paw. Then Liam smiled.

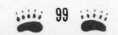

Arthur was stunned. He'd never seen Liam do a high five before. He turned to Mum and Dad. They were watching Liam and Mister P in a gooey kind of way that made Arthur want to kick something. It seemed as though Mister P and Liam were getting on brilliantly and he was being left out . . . again. He suddenly felt very alone.

'It was a good idea to bring Mister P some tea,' said Dad. 'Well done, Liam.'

'And now the rest of us need to go and have tea,' said Mum.

But Arthur didn't want any tea. He wanted to stay in the garage. He sat down on the floor opposite Mister P and gave him a serious look. Mister P gave him a serious look back.

'It was me who looked after you all day,' said Arthur. 'It was me who took you on the bus and sorted you out in the classroom and made sure you got fish and chips and chocolate ice cream for lunch. But do I get a "well done" from anyone? No, I do not.'

Mister P blinked slowly, as if he was listening to every word.

'And I'm always sticking up for Liam at school, but Mum and Dad don't see that either. It's always **Liam, Liam, Liam.**

Liam's had such a good week!

or

Liam did a beautiful painting today

or

Liam's been working so hard on his reading

'The only time they notice me is if I do something BAD. You tell me, Mister P—do you think that's fair on me?'

The bear looked steadily at Arthur and Arthur picked up a small stone from the floor and rolled it around his hand. He wanted the bear to understand.

'I wonder if you have a family somewhere, Mister P? A brother or sister maybe?'

Mister P shifted position and shuffled a little closer to Arthur.

'If you don't, you can be part of my family if you want. You and me can hang out together and have heaps of fun. Liam doesn't really like playing my kind of games and my friends don't like coming round because it can be a bit—'

Arthur sighed. How could he explain to a polar bear? It was sometimes hard trying to explain to his friends about Liam, harder still to explain to people he didn't know. Even thinking about it made his tummy hurt.

'But if you'd rather hang out with Liam then I suppose that's fine. I'll be OK.'

Arthur threw the
stone across the garage
and it clattered against
the concrete wall.
Mister P stood
up. He
padded
over to
Arthur
and he
wrapped his
paws around
him and gave
him an enor-
mous bear
hug. Arthur
stretched his
arms as far as
he could round
Mister P and
hugged him back.

A real-life, proper bear hug makes you feel better. I know because I was feeling pretty FED UP, and now I feel OK!

I didn't like watching Mister P and Liam being friends. But me and Mister P had a good chat about things and I think Mister P still likes me better than Liam—or maybe just the same.

Mister P is always nice to Liam and that makes Liam happy. And that's good, because if you are happy then it is easier to make new friends—and Liam doesn't have that many friends.

So this is what I have decided. From now on I am going to be a BETTER brother and help Liam make more friends.

CHAPTER 6
TRICKS

'You HAVE to bring Mister P to the football tournament this weekend,' said Rosie. 'Everyone loves him and he'd make a great lucky mascot for our team.'

It was Thursday morning and Rosie, Tom, and Arthur were sitting together on the bus. Mister P was getting used to the bus ride now and he lay happily on the floor between them, headphones on, listening to music.

It had been such a busy week and Arthur had been concentrating so hard on being nice that he hadn't had much time to think about the tournament this Saturday.

'I don't know if Mister P even likes football,' said Arthur. 'And how do we know he'll be lucky?'

'It won't make much difference,' said Tom. 'We never win anyway and it can't get worse than last weekend—not that I'm blaming you or anything.' Tom glanced at Arthur and Arthur's face blushed red-hot.

Last weekend's game had been a disaster. The Hawks had lost 5–1. Liam had got over-excited and sung at the top of his voice through the whole game. Arthur begged Mum to take him away from the pitch—even just a little way—but she said Liam was fine and nobody minded.

Arthur minded. How was he supposed to concentrate on saving goals with his brother making such a racket? Surely Mum could see how embarrassing it was? Every time the ball came towards Arthur's goal, Liam sang even louder and completely put Arthur off. He didn't save a single goal—not one—and that was the truth.

'I don't know if I want to play this weekend,' said Arthur.

'You have to play,' said Rosie, sounding genuinely alarmed. 'We need you—you're our best goalie.'

'I'm your *only* goalie,' said Arthur glumly.

'Come on, cheer up,' said Tom. 'At least if you bring Mister P along, we might win the prize for the best mascot.' He nudged Arthur a few times until Arthur smiled.

'Actually, there isn't a prize for best mascot,' said Elsa, butting in on their conversation. 'And anyway, I think it's illegal to have a real live bear as a lucky mascot.'

'Who cares,' said Tom. 'You don't make the rules. And you're only jealous because your team has a boring teddy bear.'

'At least our bear doesn't have bad breath.' Elsa stuck her nose in the air.

Unfortunately Elsa was a very good football player. Unfortunately she played for the Wakefield Wanderers. And unfortunately they were top of the league and they were almost guaranteed to win the tournament on Saturday.

'How would we get Mister P to the match anyway?' asked Arthur. 'He won't fit in our car.'

'I've already thought of that,' Rosie said. 'My brother can give him a lift on the back of his pick-up.'

Rosie's brother, Jonno, was a builder and in his spare time he was the Hawks' coach. His truck was dead cool.

'Could I come too?' said Arthur. He'd always wanted a ride in Jonno's truck. 'Then Mum wouldn't have to bring Liam.'

'But why don't you want to bring Liam?' said Rosie. 'He's our best supporter.'

Arthur stared at Rosie. She must be joking!

'Well, no one else comes and sings on the

sidelines in the pouring rain,' she said. 'No one else cheers us even when we play badly.'

'And not that many people cheer us when we're playing well,' laughed Tom.

'Oh, shut up,' said Rosie. 'You're not helping. Anyway, our scores are going to improve because now Mister P is going to be our lucky mascot, isn't he?' She put her hands together in the praying position. **'PLEASE.'**

'I'll think about it,' said Arthur. He wished he could be more like Tom and Rosie and not worry so much about everything all the time.

Arthur did a lot of thinking that day. He watched as Mister P helped Liam join in some of the games at break time. Soon people realized it was fun hanging out with Liam and Mister P. He watched as Mister P walked quietly with Liam to his classroom. Everything seemed better when Mister P was around—most of the time.

Arthur decided he needed to check out Mister P's football skills. If Mister P was going to be their lucky mascot—IF—then he should learn a bit about the game. So after school that afternoon, he grabbed his football from the garden shed and started *dribbling it around the garden.*

Mister P watched for a while then started
bouncing
around behind Arthur,

dodging left and right,

trying to tackle him and get the ball. He seemed
quite athletic, for a bear, and Arthur had to work
hard to keep control of the ball. It was fun.

Next Arthur
demonstrated some
keepy-uppies.
He'd been practising
all season and he liked
the idea of being able
to show off. 'You need
to keep the ball off the
ground,' he said, kicking
the ball from one foot
to the other . . .

'and then you can do it
from your knees like
this . . . and then on
your head. Oops—that
didn't exactly work,
but you get what
I mean.'

Mister P followed
every move.

'You want to try?'

Arthur tossed the
ball at Mister P. First
Mister P dribbled it
round the garden, just
as Arthur had done.
Then he stood on his
hind legs and kicked
the ball from one hairy
foot to the other . . .

six—seven—eight—nine—ten . . . then from
knee to knee . . .
eleven—twelve—
thirteen—
fourteen . . .

Arthur's jaw
nearly hit the floor
and he couldn't
help laughing. A
polar bear doing
keepy-uppies was
pretty crazy.

'Dad, Mum, Liam!' he called, as he rushed inside. 'You should see Mister P! He is AWESOME. I need to get my camera. I'm going to get a picture of this. This could be...'

Arthur was already half way up the stairs when the idea popped into his head. If he got a good picture, maybe he could enter it into the Funniest Football Photo Competition.

By the time he got back down with his camera, Dad, Mum, and Liam were in the garden where Mister P was sitting quietly with the ball in between his front paws.

Dad spread his hands. 'So? What are we supposed to be looking at?'

'You wait.' Arthur shoved his camera at Liam, picked up the ball, bounced it on his knees a few times, then kicked it towards Mister P.

'Come on—give us another demo.' Arthur prayed Mister P would do it again.

Mister P tossed the ball from foot to foot, then knee to knee, then balanced it on the end of his nose for absolutely ages. It was brilliant. Mister P was a keepy-uppy pro and would be the best lucky mascot ever. Arthur turned to grab his camera, but Liam was already snapping photo after photo.

'Give it here, Liam, quick!'

Liam kept clicking.

'Liam!' Arthur tried to grab the camera away from Liam, but Liam wouldn't let go.

'Let him hold on to it,' said Dad. 'It's keeping him happy.'

'But it's mine. It was my birthday present from Granddad. And I want to—' Arthur didn't have time to finish his sentence because Mister P headed the ball straight towards him, very hard. Arthur had to move at lightning speed to stop the ball smashing into the camera, or Liam's face, or both.

'Great save!' said Dad. 'Do that on Saturday and your team will definitely win.'

A big bubble of excitement filled Arthur's chest and he grinned at Dad. 'I hope so. The team want Mister P to be our lucky mascot. Jonno's going to collect him in his pick-up.'

'Well, having a real polar bear on the sidelines should help put all the other teams off their game!'

Arthur looked at the ground and thought for a moment. 'Does Liam have to come on Saturday?' he asked. 'I'm not being mean, but sometimes he puts me off my game—and this is a big tournament. There's going to be masses of people and it'll be noisy. Liam will hate it.'

Dad put his arm round Arthur's shoulders. 'I know it's hard sometimes,' he said. 'But Liam loves watching you play football. Imagine how unhappy he'd be if we didn't let him come?'

'But—'

Dad put his finger to Arthur's lips to stop him saying any more. 'Liam is an important part of our family. And so are you. We have to stay flexible and make things work the best we can. And that means sticking together even when things are difficult.'

'But things are always difficult,' said Arthur.

Dad gave Arthur's shoulder a squeeze. 'Is now difficult?'

Arthur looked at Mister P doing silly tricks and Liam with the camera. Mister P was posing, his hand on his hip and the ball balanced on his front paw.

'Now is OK,' he said. 'It's Saturday I'm worried about.'

CHAPTER 7
KNOTS

On Saturday morning Arthur woke up earlier than usual. He needed Mister P looking his best for the tournament. He picked up soap and toothpaste from the bathroom and the scrubbing brush they used to clean the shower. Then he grabbed a couple of towels and carried the whole lot into the garden.

He put his head round the garage door.

'Wake up, Mister P! It's time to get ready.'

Mister P yawned and stretched and followed Arthur outside. Dad's garden hose was coiled up next to the shed. Arthur turned on the tap and waited for the water to make its way through the pipe. 'It might be a bit cold,' he said, 'so watch out.'

Mister P stared at the end of the hosepipe and suddenly freezing water gushed straight into his face. Mister P spluttered and gasped and then grinned. He didn't seem to mind the cold at all. He wriggled and jiggled as Arthur sprayed him all over with water and massaged soap into his fur. He watched as rainbow soapy bubbles floated past his nose.

'Nearly done,' said Arthur, rinsing the last of the soap from Mister P's coat. Arthur turned off the tap and re-coiled the hosepipe. Mister P crouched down, winding himself up for an enormous shake.

'Noooo!', shouted Arthur, but it was too late. Mister P flung his fur left and right, sending great fountains of water across the garden.

By the time Mister P had finished, he looked as though he'd plugged his paw into an electric socket, and Arthur was soaked.

'What did you have to go and do that for?' Arthur tried to smooth the mass of fur back into place with the towels. Mister P grinned happily which made Arthur's next task easier. He smeared a whole tube of toothpaste over the scrubbing brush and set to work on Mister P's teeth. As the minty toothpaste tingled on his blue tongue, Mister P shook his head violently and went slightly cross-eyed, panting loudly and chattering his teeth together.

'Come on, it's not that bad. Don't be such a baby.'

Arthur tried again, but Mister P wrinkled up his nose and turned his head away.

'You don't want Elsa complaining that you've got bad breath, do you?'

One mention of Elsa and Mister P opened wide and let Arthur brush.

'OK, rinse and spit,' said Arthur, popping the hose into the side of Mister P's mouth.

Mister P dribbled toothpastey water onto the ground— spit, spit, spitting until every last bit of minty flavour was gone.

'DONE!' said Arthur, as he dried Mister P's muzzle and polished his nose with a towel.

Mister P flashed him a bright smile.

At one o'clock, Rosie and Jonno arrived in the pick-up truck. It had a cab at the front and a flat back, with low sides and

JW CONSTRUCTION SERVICES
—BUILDING A BETTER FUTURE

written on the side.

'See, it's perfect for transporting polar bears,' said Rosie, undoing the tailgate of the truck.

Arthur opened the double doors of the garage and Mister P emerged into the sunlight.

'Wow!' exclaimed Rosie. 'He looks amazing.'

Arthur hopped onto the back of the truck and Mister P clambered up behind him. Rosie passed Arthur her headphones and a pair of Jonno's protective eye goggles. 'For the wind,' she said. Arthur fitted the headphones over Mister P's ears and the goggles over his eyes and wrapped a green and white Hawks scarf round his neck. He gave Mister P a final check and climbed down. Jonno fixed the tailgate and gave Mister P the thumbs up.

As the truck accelerated away, Mister P raised his nose to the wind and his scarf streamed out behind him.

JW CONSTRU
—BUILDING A

TION SERVICES
BETTER FUTURE

Arthur couldn't help laughing. He wished he could be in the truck with Mister P. He wished he could have a brother like Jonno.

Liam was on the doorstep, his hands pressed over his eyes.

'It's all right, Liam. Mister P is fine. You'll see him at the football.' Arthur was keen to get going as quickly as possible and he didn't need Liam to get in a panic. But Liam wasn't looking happy at all. He kept covering and uncovering his eyes with his hands.

'What is it, Liam? You like coming to watch me play football, don't you?' Arthur tried not to sound too desperate, but it was hard. He needed Liam to get in the car. He needed to get to the tournament. Sometimes when Liam got upset, it was difficult to find out what was wrong. Arthur wished Mister P was still at home—he'd know what to do.

'Let's walk round the garden like you do with Mister P,'

suggested Arthur. He'd noticed that Liam liked walking with Mister P and it usually made things better.

Liam didn't seem sure at first, but as Arthur kept going, he started to seem calmer.

'Do you want to come to the football?' said Arthur.

Liam nodded fast.

'It starts at two o'clock.' Arthur showed Liam his watch. 'That's in thirty minutes.'

Liam nodded again.

'So we need to go.'

Liam started tapping his fingers against his eyes again. 'Camera,' he said.

'Camera?' said Arthur. 'You want to take my camera to the football?'

Liam nodded. Arthur wasn't sure he trusted Liam with his camera at the tournament, but if it was going to help get Liam into the car, that was all that mattered right now. Arthur rushed upstairs.

'OK, Liam. You promise me you'll look after it, right?'

'Right,' said Liam.

'But first we need to get in the car and get to the game or you might miss some of Mister P's football tricks. Right?'

'Right.'

Liam followed Arthur to the car, got in, and fastened his seat belt. Dad drove like a rally driver all the way to the sports field, but they were still cutting it fine.

By the time they got to the car park, it was

nearly full and there were A LOT of people.

Arthur jogged over to join his team. A large crowd had gathered around Mister P who was taking part in the team warm-up with some enthusiastic star jumps. The onlookers were clapping and cheering.

A loudspeaker crackled and squealed into life and the organizer's voice boomed out to welcome everyone to the tournament and announce the start of the first-round matches. Arthur was glad that Mister P was still wearing Rosie's headphones, but as the loudspeaker kept barking out information, he worried more and more about Liam. His brother was huddled near the side of the pitch, his hands pressed onto his ears. Arthur's tummy twisted with worry as he watched Mum trying to keep Liam calm. Arthur's camera lay discarded on the grass.

The team gathered for a pre-match huddle with Mister P at the centre. He gave each member a high five before walking off the pitch,

grinning at the supporters on the sidelines.
He was taking his role as lucky mascot very
seriously and that made Arthur worried too. If
the Hawks didn't do well, everyone might blame
Mister P—or perhaps they'd blame Arthur.
More than anything, Arthur didn't want to let
his team down. And he really, really didn't want
Liam to make a scene. Not today.

The whistle blew and the   first game
started. Now things were
under way, the shouty
screeching stopped and
Arthur noticed Mister P,
Liam, and Dad
walking slowly
round the pitch.
Every time
Arthur's team
did well, Mister P
stopped and did a
little dance.

If the Hawks lost the ball, Mister P would snarl and put his paws over his eyes.

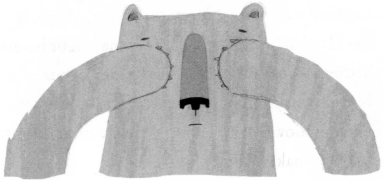

Soon the supporters got the hang of the dance and snarl routine and started to join in. Better still, Liam had the camera back in his hands and was snapping photos. Arthur started to relax a little. And when Rosie scored the first goal, he began to enjoy himself . . . and when he saved the next one, it was better still . . . and when they won the first match, it was brilliant. Mister P was dancing. Liam was dancing. And the Hawks' supporters were dancing too. Perhaps Mister P really was a lucky mascot. Perhaps nothing would go wrong at all. Arthur and the team joined Mister P to celebrate.

The loudspeaker started up again.

'WE HAVE A LOST LITTLE GIRL AT
THE OFFICIALS' TENT. PLEASE COULD
A PARENT COME AND ... *screeeeeech*
... WELL DONE, EVERYONE IN THE
FIRST MATCH. PLEASE MAKE YOUR WAY
QUICKLY... *screeeeech* ...
TO START YOUR NEXT ... *screeeech*.'

The noise was way too much for Liam. Arthur was sure he could see people edging away from his family as Liam rocked backwards and forwards, doing everything he could to block out the horrible sound. Mum was doing her best to help, but Liam was pushing her away too. Arthur clenched his hands into fists.

Rosie and Tom gave Arthur an anxious look.

'Wouldn't a pair of headphones help Liam?' asked Rosie.

'Yep, they would,' said Arthur, 'if only we could get him to wear them.'

'We could try,' said Tom.

'We've already tried.' Arthur thought of the struggles at home when Mum and Dad had tried to put anything on Liam's ears. They'd given up ages ago. Mum said it was all pointless anyway because Liam had to get used to unexpected noise. But surely not this kind of noise?

Mister P was getting restless too. He didn't like it when Liam was upset. He sat close to

Liam and swung his head from side to side. As the announcements continued, Mister P took the headphones off his own polar bear ears and held them out to Liam.

'No, no,' said Mum. 'Get those things away from him—you'll only make things worse.'

But Mister P wasn't in the mood to budge or give up trying. He put the headphones back on his own ears, blinked, and did a silly dance. Then he held them out to Liam for a second time. He repeated the same action again and again, blinking and dancing and coaxing Liam to take the headphones. By the time the last announcement squawked out over the loudspeaker, it was Liam wearing the headphones and Mister P who was covering his ears with his paws.

No one could believe it, but everyone was smiling.

'See,' said Rosie. 'Mister P knows how to get things sorted.'

Arthur gave Mister P a thumbs up.

The second game started. Liam and Mister P kept on dancing and the Hawks' supporters kept on shouting encouragement. Everyone in the team was playing their very best and Arthur was beginning to feel sure that Mister P had magical mascot powers. He seemed to be too busy razzing up all the spectators to worry about the noise. The Hawks won the second game easily and then drew the third. And that meant they'd made it to the FINAL.

'We've never made it this far before,' said Rosie nervously. 'I wonder who we'll be playing?'

'I'm guessing the **Wakefield Wanderers**,' said Tom.

There was a groan from quite a few of the

team. No one liked playing the Wanderers, mainly because Elsa was the captain and she would do *anything* to win.

The Hawks huddled together to discuss last-minute tactics, then gave Mister P a team high five. They were going to do this! Just as they broke away to run to their starting positions, Elsa said in a loud and nasty voice, 'We'll see how lucky your bear is now.'

Arthur could tell everyone was angry with her—including Mister P, who gave her a long, hard stare before prowling off the pitch.

The Wanderers were good—very good—and it was a tough game right from the start. Even so, the Hawks were just about holding their own. Dermot passed to Tom and now he was running with the ball towards goal. But just as he was about to shoot, Elsa barged into him. Tom stumbled over and fell on his face.

Everyone waited for the whistle. It *must* have been a foul! Mister P gave a loud growl and the

Hawks' supporters grumbled at the referee—but play continued and now The Wanderers had the ball.

'Come on, Tom!' shouted Rosie.

Tom was rubbing his knee as he got back to his feet. He looked upset and Arthur didn't blame him. There was no way that was a fair tackle! How could the ref have missed it? But Rosie was right—Tom needed to get back into the action or the Hawks were going to be in real trouble. The Wanderers were passing the ball forwards and Elsa ALWAYS seemed to be in the right place. Even though the others were trying, Tom was the only one who was quick enough and skilled enough to stop her.

The Hawks' supporters cheered for Tom as he raced up the pitch towards Arthur's goal. One of the Wanderers' players had just crossed the ball into the box and Elsa was set up for a shot at goal. Arthur was on **red alert**. Tom was fast—but probably not fast enough to get between Elsa and the goal. He sprinted up behind her and, realizing he had no time, flung his legs out to try and get the ball. **BAD IDEA**.

Elsa squealed and she fell to the ground, the ball trickling away from her.

The whistle blew.

PENALTY!

Arthur covered his face with his hands. He felt sorry for Tom because he could guess how he was feeling—Elsa's trip had been really unfair. But why did Tom have to go and do that? It was too risky. What was he thinking? Now Elsa was placing the ball on the spot, ready to take her penalty. And the only thing standing in the way of her scoring was Arthur. This couldn't be worse. Arthur spread his hands wide and bounced up and down, ready to spring in any direction. Meanwhile Mister P had stomped up the sideline to get as close as possible to the goal.

Arthur watched Elsa carefully as she stepped back to take her kick. He heard the sharp shrill of the whistle. He focused on the ball flying through the air. He felt it graze the tops of his fingers then tip over his head and drop into the net behind him.

'Goal!' Elsa leapt up and down with her arms in the air.

Arthur dropped to his knees and hid his face in his hands.

The Wakefield supporters cheered and the Hawks supporters clapped politely. All except Mister P. Mister P wasn't happy at all. He didn't know much about the rules of football, but he knew that this goal needed to be UN-scored. He pounded onto the pitch and headed straight for the ball at the back of Arthur's net.

POP!

went the ball as Mister P's sharp teeth sank into it.

HISSSSS!

went the air as the ball started to deflate.

Poor Mister P started to panic. More than anything, he hated the sound of hissing, and without Elsa's headphones, he couldn't get away from it. He thrashed about, trying to get the ball out of his mouth. His claws ripped at the netting of the goal, and the more he fought, the more tangled he became.

Soon he was wrapped up so tightly that he couldn't move at all.

The Wanderers stood with their arms crossed and laughed while the Hawks gathered around and tried to help.

'Look what you've done, Mister P,' said Arthur. 'We're going to be in real trouble now.'

The referee blasted on his whistle and pulled out a red card. 'Get that animal OFF the pitch!' he ordered.

'You can't send him off—he's not part of the team,' said Arthur. 'And he doesn't understand. He's a polar bear.'

'I don't care if he's a killer whale,' said the ref. 'This kind of behaviour during a tournament is totally unacceptable.'

Arthur stroked Mister P through the netting. He wished it was Elsa who was tied up. That would serve her right for tripping up Tom. It would serve her right for everything.

Rosie and Tom helped Arthur untangle the netting while Jonno went to get his tool kit from the car to fix up the goal.

When they'd finished, Mister P lay perfectly still, his fur

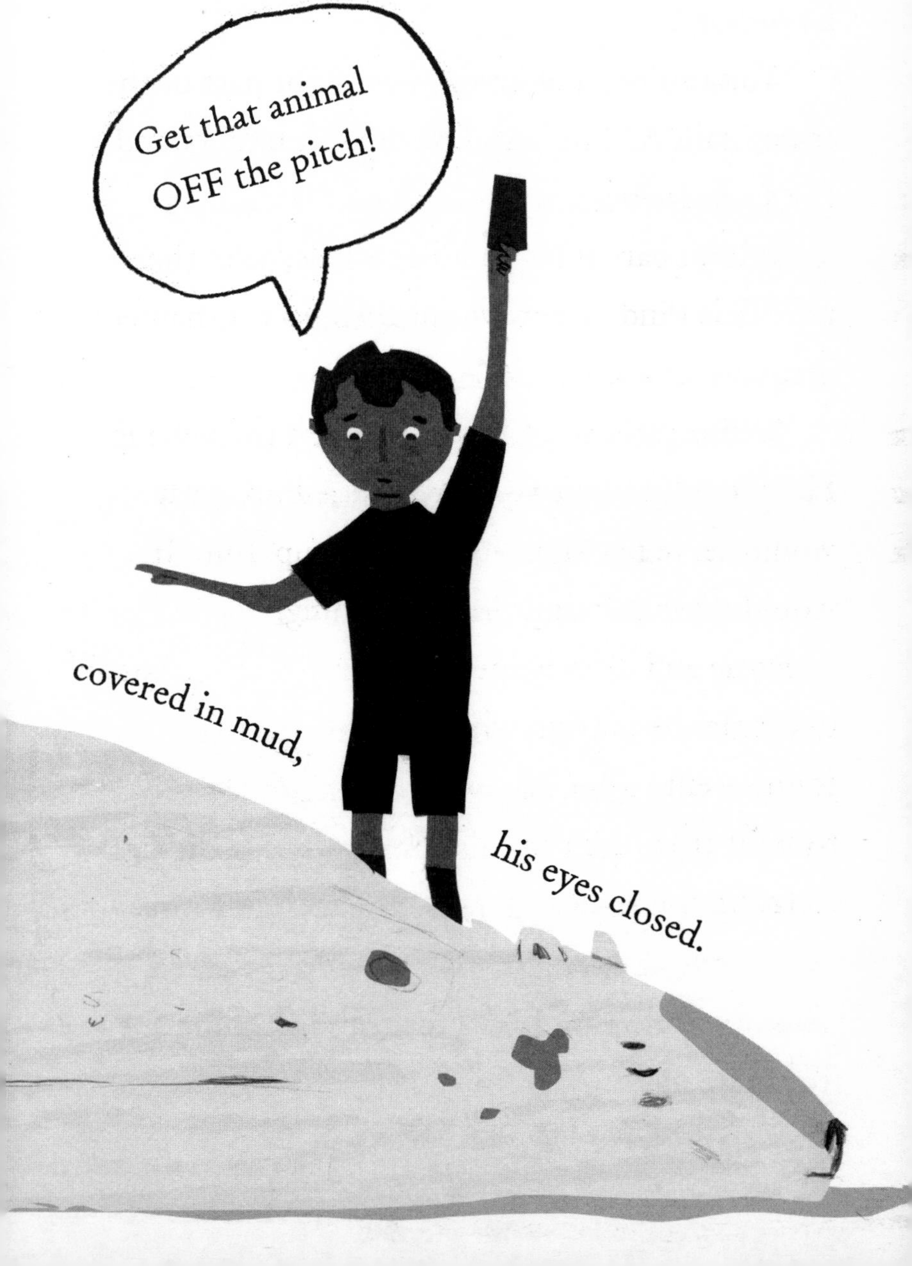

covered in mud,

his eyes closed.

'He's not dead, is he?' said Arthur.

Rosie put her ear to his heart. It was beating very fast.

'I told you he wouldn't be lucky,' said Arthur.

'It doesn't matter,' said Tom. 'It's only a game.'

But it did matter—Arthur could tell. It mattered a lot because now they were losing.

Arthur, Rosie, and Tom helped Mister P off the pitch. Liam jumped around and sang loudly, trying to make Mister P feel better, while Elsa stood with her arms crossed, whispering to her teammates.

Arthur was angry with himself and even angrier with Elsa. He wasn't going to let anything put him off his game now. He didn't care if Liam sang and danced—he didn't care what anyone thought any more. All he cared about was beating Elsa's team and winning the tournament.

Just before half time, Rosie scored a goal to make it 1–1. And then, in the second half, Tom scored to make it 2–1. All the Hawks had to do now was to hold on. Arthur wished the game would end—there couldn't be more than a few minutes left. His heart started to pound as he saw the Wanderers get the ball. He watched as they passed it up the pitch towards his goal. Now Elsa had the ball again and she was looking dangerous. Where were all the defenders? Arthur's body tensed. He focused hard on Elsa. He wasn't going to let her score. He couldn't. He mustn't.

The ball flew off her foot and came hurtling towards the corner of his goal.

Arthur launched himself off
the ground into an enormous dive.
He reached out his arm and just
managed to get his hand
to the ball and hit it away.
He'd SAVED it!

He'd actually saved it!

The final whistle blew

It was all over.

And the Hawks had won.

Arthur was swamped by all his teammates—patting him on the back and congratulating him. He heard Mum and Dad shouting from the sidelines. Then he saw the small figure of his brother running onto the pitch. He had the camera pressed to his eye and kept stopping to take photos. Finally he came right up to Arthur and put his arms tightly around his waist. Arthur thought it was the best hug he'd ever had from Liam. And the longest!

'Thank you, Liam,' said Arthur, laughing. 'You can let go now.'

But Liam couldn't hear a thing because he was still wearing Rosie's headphones. Arthur didn't really care. After everything that had happened with Mister P, he didn't think he'd ever get embarrassed again. So he let Liam carry on clinging as he searched around for Mister P. Where was he? Arthur was sure he'd been on the pitch at the end of the game, but now there was no sign of him anywhere.

'YOUR ATTENTION, PLEASE!' screeched the loudspeaker.

'COULD THE OWNERS OF A LARGE POLAR BEAR PLEASE MAKE THEIR WAY TO THE ICE-CREAM VAN AS QUICKLY AS POSSIBLE. THIS IS AN EMERGENCY!'

Arthur's eyes widened. He pulled Liam's arms away and ran as fast as he could towards the far end of the playing fields. Dad and Rosie and Tom ran with him. Before they got anywhere near the van, they heard a terrible commotion. A huge crowd was standing in a semicircle around the side of the van and they were shouting and laughing. Arthur pushed his way through. He emerged into the space in front of the crowd to find it littered with napkins and lollies and goodness knows what else.

'Mister P, what are you doing?' yelled Arthur, dodging a plastic lid as it flew through the air. Mister P had his snout plunged into a large tub of chocolate ice cream and, judging by the number of empty ice-cream tubs lying around him, this wasn't his first.

'Mister P!' said Dad fiercely.

Mister P lifted his head and grinned. Ice cream dripped off his nose and his normally white teeth were now coated in dark brown.

Arthur tried hard to stop himself from laughing. This was a serious situation.

Dad attempted to pull the tub away from Mister P, but Mister P held on tight and sank his nose back into the lovely, cold chocolatey mess. Arthur snorted with laughter—he couldn't help it—and quickly covered his mouth with his hand, pretending to cough.

The ice-cream lady stood at the window of her van, looking very flustered. 'You need to teach that bear some manners,' she said. 'He must learn to wait to be served. He's eaten half my supplies already. And what he hasn't eaten, he's just thrown away. You'll have to pay for this, you know—and if you don't get him away from my van right away,

I'm going to call the police.' She held her mobile phone in the air and waved it around.

Arthur stopped laughing and tried to get Mister P to move. Dad hurried over to the window, his wallet in his hand.

Mister P stopped guzzling.

'That is quite enough ice cream for one day, Mister P,' said Arthur, kicking the now-empty tub out of the way. 'Eat any more and your teeth will rot.'

Mister P's eyebrows twitched.

'I'm not lying,' said Arthur. 'You can ask anyone. And what's more, you need to leave some for everyone else. You're not the only person who likes ice cream, you know.'

Mister P hung his head and looked hopefully at the ice-cream van.

Jonno was now standing in the queue behind Dad. 'Talking of ice creams,' he said, 'I think the whole team deserves a treat and I'm buying.'

The Hawks all
cheered
and even the ice-cream lady gave
a small smile—she seemed to have
calmed down a little. She counted
out the money Dad had given her
and stuffed it in her cash box before
serving Jonno. He passed out ice-
cream cones to all the team and there
was one left over.

'This one is for Liam,' said Jonno.
'For being such a good supporter.'

Liam was busy snapping photos of
Mister P. The greedy bear was licking
every last drop of chocolate off the
fur around his mouth. Arthur took
the ice cream from Jonno and carried
it over to Liam.

'Here you are, Liam,' said Arthur. 'This is especially for you. Jonno says thank you for being our best supporter.'

Liam smiled.

'*Don't* let Mister P eat it,' Arthur added, 'or he might be sick.'

It was true, Mister P was starting to look a bit green, which is difficult for a polar bear, but that didn't seem to stop him from gazing hopefully at Liam.

'NO!' said Liam firmly and turned his back on Mister P.

Mister P lay down on the grass and moaned quietly.

'I think we should give three cheers for our lucky mascot,' said Jonno. 'Hip, hip . . .'

'Hooray, hooray, hooray!' shouted the team.

CHAPTER 8
SNAPS

On the way home, Liam turned Arthur's camera over and over in his hands. It was beginning to get irritating.

'You can give me the camera back now, if you want,' said Arthur.

Liam did not want.

'I only lent it to you—you can't keep it. Tell him, Dad.'

'Let's try and get home without an argument,' said Dad. 'We'll sort the camera later.'

Arthur pressed his lips together and stared out of the back window. Jonno and Rosie were

close behind in the truck and, once they'd all arrived home, Arthur waited outside to help unload Mister P. He wasn't looking quite as sleek and clean as he had that morning. His fur was messy and matted and had a grassy-green tinge to it. He was spattered with mud, or possibly chocolate ice cream—it was hard to tell.

'See you on Monday,' said Rosie, waving.

Mister P lifted a paw, then plodded back to the garage and lay down. Arthur sat cross-legged on the floor beside him and stroked his head.

'I think you might have eaten a bit too much ice cream,' he said. 'Don't worry, you'll soon feel better.'

Mister P groaned and Arthur chuckled.

'Thanks for trying to help today. I know you thought Elsa tripped up Tom on purpose. That's what we all thought. But the thing is, if the ref doesn't see, there's not a lot you can do—and, for future reference, you can't run onto the pitch in the middle of a game, and you can't un-score a goal.'

Mister P blinked three times.

'But you were great with Liam. Maybe Rosie's right, maybe he is our best supporter. I suppose it doesn't matter if he does weird stuff—as long as he's happy. Once people get to know him they know it's just Liam being Liam. I only care because he's my brother. I can't help that, can I?'

Mister P rested his nose on his paws and Arthur propped his chin on his hands.

'It's only stupid people like Elsa who like to make trouble and I've decided Elsa isn't worth worrying about any more. Especially now we've beaten her team!'

The bear lifted his head and rubbed his cool, wet nose against Arthur's nose.

Arthur smiled. 'Did you know your nose smells of chocolate, Mister P?'

Mister P went slightly cross-eyed and gave his nose a lick, just in case.

'You can't be feeling that bad,' said Arthur. 'Not if you're still searching for leftovers!'

'Arthur!' Dad called from the house. 'Do you want to come and look at Liam's photos? He's downloading them onto my computer. Then you can have your camera back.'

Arthur was exhausted, but he wanted his camera back and he was interested to see what Liam had been up to. Plus he bet Mister P had never seen photos of himself before.

'Come on,' said Arthur. 'I've got something to show you. You'll love it.'

Mister P heaved himself to his feet and followed Arthur to the door of the living room. Dad looked at the two of them and frowned. 'I'm not sure it's a good idea to bring Mister P in here. He's bound to knock something over— in fact he'll probably knock everything over.'

'But he wants to see the pictures.'

Liam bounced up and down on his chair and clapped his hands together.

'Mister P,

'Mister P,'
                        he chanted.

'All right, all right,' said Mum. 'I'm sure if we move a few things, we can manage.'

Dad rolled his eyes. Mum and Arthur shifted a couple of table lamps and moved Mum's little collection of china birds. Dad pushed a chair out of the way to make more space, then the whole family, including Mister P, gathered round the screen.

'How many photos are there?' Mum asked. 'They're taking for ever to download.'

'One hundred and fifty-seven,' said Dad.

Arthur gasped. 'Crikey, Liam! A hundred and fifty-seven? That's crazy.'

Liam was focused on the computer. He liked computers. He hit the button and started clicking through the photos.

An image of Mister P filled the screen. Mister P jumped back in surprise then stared at the picture of the polar bear and growled.

'It's you, you silly bear,' said Arthur.

Mister P swung his head from side to side as if he was face-to-face with his worst enemy.

'Hey, take it easy,' said Dad.

When the next photo appeared, Mister P screwed his eyes tight shut and then opened them again. He stretched forward and started sniffing round behind the screen, nearly knocking it onto the floor.

'There's nothing there!' Arthur said, lifting up the monitor and putting it down again, just to prove his point. 'It's a picture. It's not real. Liam took these photos of you doing keepy-uppies. Don't you remember?'

Mister P sat down and blinked a few times. His nose twitched, and as photo after photo appeared on the screen, he started to grin.

'You're quite photogenic, Mister P,' said Mum, laughing.

Liam kept going. Now the photos were of Mister P at the football tournament. First there were a few of Mister P dancing on the sidelines, then some of him pounding onto the pitch after Elsa's goal, then sinking his teeth into the ball. When they got to the photos of Mister P tangled in netting, Mister P covered his eyes, gave a loud snort, and dived behind the chair, hiding his head under a cushion.

'Goodness,' said Dad. 'Someone's sensitive.'

Arthur bent down and lifted the corner of Mister P's cushion. 'It's all right. There's no need to get your fur in a fuzz. We can delete any photos you don't like. Come and look at the rest.'

But Mister P's fur was in a fuzz and he wasn't the slightest bit interested in looking at any more pictures—not even the funny ones. Instead, he kept his head turned away from the screen and slunk back to the garage. Arthur was about to go after him, but Mum put out her hand.

'Leave him be for a while,' she said. 'Polar bears are normally quite solitary creatures. I think he's had enough excitement for one day.'

Arthur shrugged. He glanced towards the door. He didn't like to think of Mister P being unhappy.

Dad and Liam finished flicking through the photos. Liam disconnected the camera, handed it to Arthur, hopped off his chair, and walked out of the room.

'Between Liam and Mister P, they've certainly given us some entertainment today,' said Dad. He started swiping back through the photos and Arthur sat down beside him. Before long the two of them were doubled up, laughing.

'Some of these are so funny,' said Dad. 'Just look at this one . . . and this one!' Dad paused at a photo of Mister P balancing the ball on the end of his nose. 'I mean this is the kind of photo we could enter into that Funniest Football Photo Competition. Who else will have a photo of a polar bear doing tricks with a football? It's completely unique— and it'll make everyone laugh!'

Arthur's mouth opened in amazement. Had Dad just said what he thought he'd said? 'Can we?' he begged. 'Can we really? It's not too late, but we'll have to be quick. The competition closes tomorrow—I remember them saying last week. We could win tickets to the

Arthur started singing and swaying from side to side on the chair.

'One thing at a time,' said Dad. 'Just because we enter, it doesn't mean we win.'

'But we might,' said Arthur. 'Someone's got to.'

Dad grinned.

'And going to the cup final would be ACE,' said Arthur.

'It would be fun—especially with a polar bear,' said Dad. 'But don't tell anyone for now. It's going to be our secret.'

CHAPTER 9
COUNTDOWN

YOUR ENTRY
HAS BEEN RECEIVED.

THE WINNER
WILL BE NOTIFIED BY EMAIL

AT 12 NOON
ON SATURDAY.

'There we go,' said Dad. 'Now all we have to do is wait.'

Arthur couldn't take his eyes from the screen. How could he wait a whole seven days? He didn't even know how he was going to get through the next seven hours—or even seven minutes. Imagine if they won? He could picture Mister P arriving at the cup final in his City scarf. Maybe he'd turn out to be a lucky mascot for City too?

He was busting to tell someone. Perhaps he could mention it to Mister P because Mister P wouldn't tell a soul. Or maybe he shouldn't. Maybe he should wait and see if they won the tickets and if they did (which they wouldn't) but IF they did, then he could give Mister P the best surprise of his life.

Arthur danced towards the garage to check on his grumpy bear. He hoped Mister P would have forgotten about the embarrassing photos by now. Did polar bears have a good memory, he wondered. Before he even opened the door, Arthur could hear Mister P snoring at top

volume. He crept in quietly and watched
the peaceful polar bear for a few minutes.
The real Mister P was better than any
photo.

'Goodnight, Mister P,' he whispered.
'Sleep tight. Hope the spiders don't
bite.' Arthur smiled and closed the
door without making a sound.

He ran to his room, picked up his lucky crystal, and made a wish. 'I wish to win the Funniest Football Photo Competition,' he said. He put his lucky crystal under his pillow. Now his lips were sealed. He wouldn't tell Tom or Rosie or anyone because Mum always said that if you tell someone what you wish for then you don't get it.

He could tell his journal, though—surely that wouldn't count? And he reckoned he needed to do *something* to get him through the next week! So he pulled it out from its secret hiding place and opened it to a blank page. He wrote

COMPETITION COUNTDOWN

at the top of the page, then

TOP SECRET

underneath. Looking at the empty pages ahead gave him a horrible feeling that this was going to be the l o n g e s t seven days in the history of the universe.

On Sunday the whole family went to Liam's favourite place—The Museum of Flying.

On Monday Dad bought Liam and Mister P identical headphones to Rosie's.

On Tuesday, I persuaded Mum and Dad
to let Liam come to school on the bus.

On Wednesday, after school, Mum took me, Liam, and Mister P to the local street market.

On Thursday, it was Liam's birthday.

All he wanted was his very own football— so that's what I gave him.

On Friday, me, Liam, and Mister P
were given a prize in school assembly
for 'good work' on the Arctic topic.

ONE MORE SLEEP!

TOMORROW IS THE BIG DAY.

AHHHHHHHHHHHHHHH.

On Saturday morning Arthur woke up with butterflies fluttering in his stomach. It was either going to be the best day ever—or the worst. Arthur wondered what else he could do to bring himself luck. He put his pants on back to front and his T-shirt inside out—he was sure Granddad had told him that was lucky. He finished getting dressed, put his lucky crystal in his pocket, and ran downstairs.

Liam was in the garden with Mister P. Mum was reading the paper and Dad was making breakfast.

'Have you checked your emails?' asked Arthur.

Dad smiled. 'I think it's a bit early for that, don't you?' Dad gave Arthur a wink so Mum couldn't see. Arthur squeezed his eyes and fists tight shut to try to stop the excitement from bursting out of him.

The morning dragged by. For once it was Liam who was calm and Arthur who couldn't keep still. Dad took them to the park, but Arthur didn't feel like playing. He walked three times round the pond with Mister P and then watched Liam going backwards and forwards, backwards and forwards on the swing about a thousand times. Liam refused to get off, so there was a bit of a scene and he ended up riding all the way home on Mister P's back. By the time they reached the front door, it was just seven minutes before twelve o'clock.

Arthur rushed into the living room and switched on the computer, then he and Dad hunched side by side, close to the screen.

'Now, you're not to be disappointed if we don't win,' Dad whispered.

Arthur gave his head a little shake.

'Our chances of winning are almost zero.' Dad held his finger and thumb in an '0' shape.

'*Almost,*' said Arthur, as he scanned the unread emails in Dad's mailbox. It was boring stuff. There was nothing mentioning 'cup final' or 'winner'. He knew the sound Dad's computer made every time a new email came in and he waited for that magic 'ping'. The silence stretched and stretched and stretched. Arthur checked his watch and fiddled with the crystal in his pocket. Thirty seconds to go until twelve o'clock . . . twenty . . . ten. He closed his eyes and crossed his fingers.

Come on!
Come on!

Ping!

The noise was tiny, but Arthur nearly fell off his chair. Dad had his hand over his mouth as he opened the email.

CONGRATULATIONS!

Arthur's brain was fizzing.

'I don't believe it!' Dad gasped. He raked his hand through his hair and squinted at the email again. Then he leapt to his feet. Dad and Arthur danced round and round in circles.

'We won, we won, we won!'

Three tickets to the cup final. Chauffeur-driven car. Meet the team. This was beyond Arthur's wildest dreams. Just wait until he told Mister P.

Mum appeared in the doorway. 'What's happened?' she said. 'Have we won the lottery?'

'Better,' said Arthur. 'We've won the Funniest Football Photo Competition!' Arthur ran on the spot at top speed. 'We entered a photo of Mister P.'

Mum looked at Dad and Dad shrugged. 'We thought it would be a laugh,' said Dad. 'We never expected to win. But we have—come and look!'

Mum was completely stunned. She gave Arthur a quick hug and then leant forward to check the email. She laughed. 'Tickets to the cup final. That's incredible!'

'I have to go and tell Mister P,' said Arthur.

'Hang on,' said Mum, holding Arthur by the hand. She was reading over the email again.

'What's the matter,' said Arthur.

'You've won *three* tickets?' said Mum. 'I'm just wondering who is going to go?'

Dad looked at Mum.

'There has to be an adult,' said Dad. 'So I guess that's me, given that you're not that keen on the footie. So then I'll take Arthur and Mister P.'

'But what about Liam?' said Mum. 'After all, he took the photo. It hardly seems fair to leave him out of this.'

Arthur stopped jiggling. His excitement faded a little.

'We can't really take Liam, can we?' said Dad. 'Let's face it, he'd really struggle to deal with the crowds and the noise. The cup final is huge.'

Mum looked out of the window where Liam was trying to play football with Mister P.

'I seem to remember we said he would struggle with a polar bear, or wearing headphones or going to school on the bus,' she said, 'but he seems to be finding ways to cope with lots of things these days. We've always said we must keep things fair with the boys. I don't want to be the one to explain to Liam that he's being left behind while you go off and watch his favourite team play in the final.'

Arthur looked at his feet. 'But if Dad takes Liam and me, then what about Mister P?'

The room filled with a polar-bear-sized silence. 'We can't leave him out. Without Mister P we wouldn't have a photograph at all. That doesn't seem fair either.'

'You should have thought about all this before entering,' said Mum. 'You must've known it was only three tickets.'

'We didn't exactly anticipate winning,' said Dad, raising his voice. Arthur hated it when Mum and Dad argued.

Mum crossed her arms with a thump. 'Well, now we have a problem, don't we?'

Arthur didn't want to look at Mum or Dad. He wanted this problem to go away. Mum crouched down in front of him and put her hands on his shoulders. 'I'm sorry, Arthur,' she said. 'I know how excited you are—we just need to work out what to do, that's all.'

'I'm going to talk to Mister P,' said Arthur. 'He'll know what to do.'

Arthur stomped out of the living room just as his brother tiptoed his way in. Liam must have heard them arguing because he was doing his upset thing, rocking backwards and forwards. 'All right, Liam?' said Arthur. He knew better than to expect an answer.

Arthur marched into the garage and slammed the door. Mister P looked at him warily. Arthur took a deep breath.

'I've come to tell you that we've won three tickets to the cup final,' he said, trying to sound happy. 'Dad and I entered a photo of you into the Funniest Football Photo Competition. I kept it a secret because I wanted to give you a nice surprise.'

Mister P tipped his head on one side and listened.

'I've decided that you and Liam can go with Dad—because otherwise it wouldn't be fair.' Even as the words tumbled out of Arthur's mouth, he felt sick with jealousy.

Mister P sat down.

'You're supposed to be excited,' said Arthur. 'Don't you understand? This is like the best thing that could ever happen.'

Mister P hardly reacted at all and Arthur felt so frustrated he kicked the nearest thing he could see—which happened to be Mister P's suitcase. It fell over with a THUNK and hurt Arthur's toe.

'And why have you got your suitcase in the middle of the floor?' Arthur went to pick it up and return it to the shelf, but it was so heavy he could barely lift it. And it smelt faintly fishy. Arthur started to feel uneasy. Something wasn't right.

Mister P lifted his big dark eyes to Arthur's face and Arthur thought he could see tears creeping down the fur on Mister P's nose.

'Mister P?'

Mister P blinked three times and held out a claw towards Arthur. Hanging on the end of it was the address label from his suitcase.

29 Ellis Street

Arthur smiled. 'Oh, is that the problem? Your label has come off. Don't worry, I'll have that tied back on in a nanosecond.' Arthur bent down and his smile changed to a frown. There was already a label on Mister P's suitcase. A new label. A label that said

Hazeldown Farm

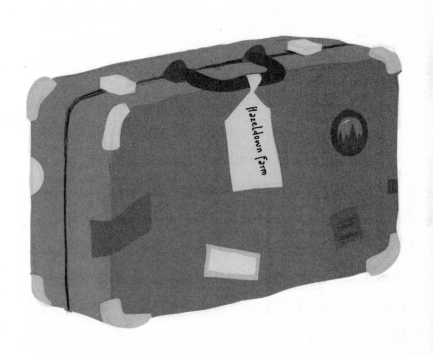

As far as Arthur knew, there were no farms anywhere near here.

Arthur flung his arms around the bear's neck. **'Oh, Mister P!** Did you hear us arguing about those stupid tickets? Families get like that sometimes—or mine does anyway. You don't need to worry. We don't want you to leave or anything.'

Mister P picked up the suitcase in his mouth and stood facing Arthur.

Arthur moved fast, pressing his back to the door. 'Don't be silly. Go and put your suitcase back on the shelf and I'll get you some chocolate ice cream.'

Mister P took a step forward and waited. Arthur had a bad feeling about this. A very bad feeling indeed.

'You can't leave us Mister P! No way! I don't know where this farm place is, but you are not going there, or anywhere. This is your home now.'

Mister P stood very still. He didn't even blink. He stared into Arthur's eyes and Arthur stared back and suddenly Arthur knew for sure . . . Mister P really was leaving. He tried to speak, but the words wouldn't get past the lump in his throat. Big, fat tears rolled down his face and Mister P licked them away as gently as he could with his rough blue tongue.

'Have you ever been to a farm before? They're for cows and sheep and pigs. They are not for polar bears.

Are you listening to me?'

Mister P blinked three times, placed his paw on Arthur's shoulder, and smiled. They stood for a few moments, face-to-face, until Arthur managed a wobbly smile back.

Something in Arthur's head told him he had to let Mister P go. If the bear had made up his mind, there was no way Arthur, or anyone else, would be able to stop him.

Arthur opened the garage door and stood to one side. He walked with Mister P through the hall, to the front door of the house. It felt like only yesterday that Mister P had come crashing into this hallway—and into his life. Mum and Dad and Liam were in the living room and Arthur could hear Liam making happy rocket noises.

Mister P put his paw to his lips, as if to say 'shhhhhhh'.

Arthur tried to cry silently, his chin wobbling as he swallowed down the sobs. His hand shook as he undid the latch on the front door and opened it wide.

'Goodbye, Mister P,' he whispered. 'I can't believe you're really going to go.'

Mister P touched his damp nose against

Arthur's damp nose, then stood up and took one step out of the house. He paused for a moment to sniff the air, his huge, hairy body filling the whole doorway. Then he walked away down the street, his suitcase in his hand.

CHAPTER 10
SNIFF

Arthur was in shock. He didn't want to speak to anyone so he went straight back to the garage and sat down. The space felt large and empty and abandoned. He picked up a thin strand of polar bear fur from the floor and twiddled it in his fingers. He sat until his bum went numb. He sat until Mum came in and gave him a hug. It was a hug that told Arthur that Mum knew something was very wrong.

'Mister P has gone,' said Arthur.

'Gone?' said Mum. 'Are you sure?'

Arthur shrugged miserably. 'He had a

new label on his suitcase. It said Hazeldown Farm.

'Ah,' said Mum. She looked around the empty garage and sighed.

'Do you know where Hazeldown Farm is?' asked Arthur.

'Not exactly. But I have a feeling that it may be somewhere where only a polar bear will do.' Arthur wiped his eyes with the back of his sleeve and sniffed. He wasn't sure he understood what Mum meant. 'He will come back, won't he?'

Mum squeezed Arthur a little tighter. 'No. I'm not sure he will.'

'Did you tell him to go?' Arthur said, pushing Mum away in horror.

Mum shook her head. 'I don't think anyone can tell Mister P what to do. He just knows.'

Arthur frowned as he tried to sort out the jumble of thoughts in his head.

'Did I do something wrong then?'

Mum knelt on the floor in front of Arthur and took his hands in hers. 'No, you didn't do anything wrong. You looked after him brilliantly. You were a good friend for Mister P and he was a good friend for you. Look at the adventures you had and all the things we've learned. I think he just realized you didn't need him around any more. It was time for him to go and knock on someone else's door. Someone who needed him even more than you.'

'Liam needs him more than me.'

'But Mister P knows that you're going to look after each other now.'

And just at that moment, the door creaked open and Liam walked in. He sat down next to Arthur, legs almost touching.

'You loved that bear too, didn't you?' said Arthur.

Liam hugged his arms across his chest and rocked slowly backwards and forwards. For once

Arthur thought he knew just how Liam
was feeling.

'It looks like it's you and me now,' said
Arthur. 'I think that's how Mister P wanted it
to be.'

Liam carried on rocking and Arthur wished
he could do something to cheer him up.

'Would you like to come to the cup final with me and Dad? I don't mean watch it on the TV,

I mean
actually
GO.'

Liam stopped rocking.

'Arthur,' said Mum in a warning voice. 'We should probably discuss this first.'

'I am,' said Arthur. 'With Liam. You like watching the football, don't you? It'll be just like the tournament, except a bit bigger—and a bit more crowded—and maybe a bit noisier. But heaps of fun. More fun than any other football match you've ever seen. You can take your headphones and my camera and we can sing all our favourite football songs.'

Liam started to hum.

'Arthur!' said Mum.

'No point in wasting a ticket,' said Arthur. 'No point in Mister P leaving for nothing.'

Arthur raised his hand and held it out to
Liam. 'High five?'

'High five,' said Liam.

'I hope you two know what you're doing,'
said Mum.

CHAPTER 11
HOORAY!

The football stadium was packed. Arthur, Liam, and Dad sat in their special seats.

Arthur had his lucky crystal in his pocket. It made him feel close to Mister P.

Liam had his headphones clamped on his ears and Arthur's camera in his hand, and he was humming at top volume. But he was OK—for the moment.

The announcer's voice rang out around the stadium:

'We'd like to give a special welcome to our Funniest Football Photo competition winners —Liam and Arthur Mallows with their winning photo of Mister P.'

A picture of Mister P doing keepy-uppies burst onto the big screen. A huge cheer went round the stadium and all around them people laughed and clapped. Arthur gave Liam a gentle nudge and pointed at the screen.

At the sight of Mister P, Liam leapt to his feet and started to dance. The camera panned in on the VIP seats where Liam and Arthur were sitting and suddenly it was Liam and Arthur on the big screen. Arthur blushed and tugged at Liam's shirt to make him sit down, but Liam was enjoying himself far too much. And what did it matter anyway? Arthur leapt off his seat and danced too.

As the teams ran onto the pitch, a huge cheer went up. Arthur looked at Liam as he hopped from foot to foot. Maybe it would be boring having an ordinary brother. An extraordinary brother was much more exciting—most of the time.

The whistle blew.
The match started.
And Arthur hoped that
Mister P could see . . .
wherever he might be!

Liam and me, we still miss Mister P.
If I could write a letter to him then this is
what I would say:

Dear Mister P

Thank you for coming to stay. We wish you were still here and we miss you A LOT. I hope you are happy at Hazeldown Farm, but I don't think you will like it as much as 29 Ellis Street so I have left your things in the garage in case you want to come back. I think the spiders are missing you too (HA, HA—that was a joke by the way).

Me, Liam, and Dad had a great time at the football. They showed the winning photo of you on the big screen—you should have seen it.

Please come back and see us one day.

Love Arthur

XO

(touching noses)   (bear hug)

PS Liam is coming on the bus to school every day now.
PPS Elsa has invited me to her birthday party! (I haven't decided yet whether to go—what do you think?)
PPPS I wish I could send you this letter.

Then Arthur closed his journal and put it back in its very secret hiding place.

ABOUT THE AUTHOR

Maria Farrer lives in a house in the middle of a field in
Somerset with her husband and her very spoilt dog. She
used to live on a small farm in New Zealand with a flock
of sheep, a herd of cows, two badly-behaved pigs, and a
budgie that sat on her head while she wrote. She trained
as a speech therapist and teacher and later she completed
an MA in Writing for Young people. She loves language
and enjoys reading and writing books for children of all
ages. She likes to ride her bike to the top of steep hills so
she can hurtle back down again as fast as possible. She
also loves mountains, snow, and adventure and one day
she dreams of going to the Arctic to see polar bears in
the wild.

ABOUT THE ILLUSTRATOR

Daniel Rieley is a British freelance illustrator based in Lisbon. After studying at The Arts Institute Bournemouth, undertaking an epic backpacking adventure in Australia, and working for three years in London, he decided to take off to sunny Portugal. For the past few years, Daniel has been working on several illustration projects from advertising, print, and card design to children's books.

When Daniel is not drawing, you can probably find him trying to catch waves, taking photos with old cameras, or playing his newly discovered sport, Padel.

AMAZING POLAR BEARS

Polar bears might look white, but their fur is actually transparent. Thick, hollow hairs reflect light to give the bear its white-looking coat—excellent camouflage for the snowy environment.

🐾Under all that fur, polar bears have dark bluey-black skin which helps them to absorb the sun's heat. They also have bluey-black tongues!

🐾 Polar bears are so well adapted for the cold Arctic environment that often they will get too hot and have to roll around in the snow to cool off.

Polar bears have huge roughly textured paws measuring up to thirty centimetres across. The size helps to distribute their weight on thin ice, and the coarse surface acts like tread on a shoe, to stop them from slipping.

Nose-to-nose greetings are the way one polar bear will ask another for something, like food.

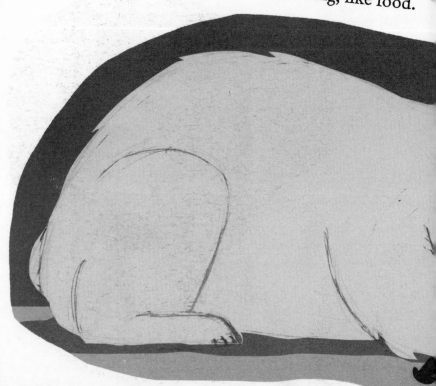

Most polar bears sleep for seven to eight hours at a stretch and they take naps too. In that way, they're very human.

A newborn polar bear cub weighs roughly the same amount as an adult guinea pig.

Here are some other stories we think

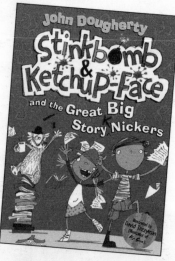